# AQA Science
## Physics

**Revision Guide**

New GCSE

D0177037

**Pauline Anning**

Series Editor
**Lawrie Ryan**

Nelson Thornes

AQA examination questions are reproduced by permission of the Assessment and Qualifications Alliance.

Published in 2011 by:
Nelson Thornes Ltd
Delta Place
27 Bath Road
CHELTENHAM
GL53 7TH
United Kingdom

11 12 13 14 15 / 10 9 8 7 6 5 4 3 2 1

A catalogue record for this book is available from the British Library

ISBN 978 1 4085 0834 3

Cover photograph: iStockphoto (background); David Deas/Getty Images (boy)

Page make-up by Wearset Ltd, Boldon, Tyne and Wear

Printed in China by 1010 Printing International Limited

**Photo acknowledgements**
Page 1 Martyn F. Chillmaid.

**Unit 1**
P1.1.7 iStockphoto; P1.1.8 Olsberg; P1.3.2 ChinaFotoPress/Getty Images; P1.3.3 (top) iStockphoto; P1.3.3 (bottom) Martyn F. Chillmaid/Science Photo Library; P1.4.2 (top) Skyscan/Science Photo Library; P1.4.2 (bottom) Canada Press/PA Photos; P1.5.4 Photolibrary/Peter Arnold Images; P1.6.5 Mark Garlick/Science Photo Library.

**Unit 2**
P2.2.7 iStockphoto; P2.3.5 AFP/Getty Images; P2.3.7 Fstop/Getty Images; P2.5.2 iStockphoto; P2.5.3 Fotolia; P2.5.4 Cordelia Molloy/Science Photo Library; P2.7.4 NASA/NOAO/AURA/NSF/T. Rector and B.A. Wolpa.

**Unit 3**
P3.3.1 Cordelia Molloy/Science Photo Library.

# Physics　Contents

# Welcome to AQA GCSE Physics!

## Key points

At the start of each topic are the important points that you must remember.

This book has been written for you by the people who will be marking your exams, very experienced teachers and subject experts. It covers everything you need to revise for your exams and is packed full of features to help you achieve the very best that you can.

Key words are highlighted in the text and are shown **like this**. You can look them up in the glossary at the back of the book if you're not sure what they mean.

 Where you see this icon, you will know that this topic involves How Science Works – a really important part of your GCSE.

IIII➡ *These questions check that you understand what you're learning as you go along. The answers are all at the back of the book.*

**Many diagrams are as important for you to learn as the text, so make sure you revise them carefully.**

Anything in the Higher boxes must be learned by those sitting the Higher Tier exam. If you're sitting the Foundation Tier, these boxes can be missed out.

The same is true for any other places that are marked [**H**].

*Higher*

## AQA *Examiner's tip*

AQA Examiner's tips are hints from the examiners who will mark your exams, giving you important advice on things to remember and what to watch out for.

## *Bump up your grade*

How you can improve your grade – this feature shows you where additional marks can be gained.

## *Maths skills*

This feature highlights the maths skills that you will need for your Science exams with short, visual explanations.

At the end of each chapter you will find:

# End of chapter questions

These questions will test you on what you have learned throughout the whole chapter, helping you to work out what you have understood and where you need to go back and revise.

And at the end of each unit you will find:

# AQA Examination-style questions

These questions are examples of the types of questions you will answer in your actual GCSE, so you can get lots of practice during your course.

You can find answers to the End of chapter and AQA Examination-style questions at the back of the book.

Student Book
pages 24–25

**P1**

# 1.1  Infrared radiation

## Key points

- Infrared radiation is energy transfer by electromagnetic waves.
- All objects emit infrared radiation.
- The hotter an object is the more infrared radiation it emits in a given time.

**AQA** *Examiner's tip*

Remember that the transfer of energy by infrared radiation does **not** involve particles.

- Infrared waves are part of the electromagnetic spectrum. They are the part of the spectrum just beyond visible red light. We can detect **infrared radiation** with our skin – it makes us feel warm.
- All objects **emit** (give off) infrared radiation.
- The hotter an object is the more infrared radiation it emits in a given time.

▸ **1**  *How does the temperature of an object affect the rate at which it emits infrared radiation?*

- Infrared radiation can travel through a vacuum, as in travelling through space. This is how we get energy from the Sun.

▸ **2**  *What is a vacuum?*

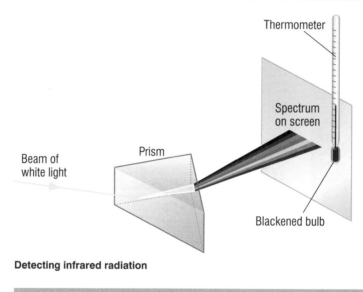

Thermometer

Spectrum on screen

Beam of white light

Prism

Blackened bulb

**Detecting infrared radiation**

**Key words:** infrared radiation, emit

Student Book
pages 26–27

**P1**

# 1.2  Surfaces and radiation

## Key points

- Dark, matt surfaces emit infrared radiation more quickly than light, shiny surfaces.
- Dark, matt surfaces absorb infrared radiation more quickly than light, shiny surfaces.
- Light, shiny surfaces reflect more infrared radiation than dark, matt surfaces.

- Dark, matt surfaces are good **absorbers** of infrared radiation. An object painted dull black and left in the Sun will become hotter than the same object painted shiny white.

▸ **1**  *Why are houses in hot countries often painted white?*

- Dark, matt surfaces are also good **emitters** of infrared radiation. So an object that is painted dull black will transfer energy and cool down more quickly than the same object painted shiny white.

▸ **2**  *Why are the pipes on the back of a fridge usually painted black?*

- Light, shiny surfaces are good **reflectors** of infrared radiation.

**Key words:** absorber, emitter, reflector

Student Book
pages 28–29 **P1**

# 1.3 States of matter

- The three states of matter are **solid**, **liquid** and **gas**. We can make a substance change between these states by heating or cooling it.
- In a solid, the particles vibrate about fixed positions so the solid has a fixed shape.
- In a liquid, the particles are in contact with each other but can move about at random, so a liquid doesn't have a fixed shape and can flow.

> **1** *How is the arrangement of the particles in a liquid different from that in a solid?*

- In a gas, the particles are usually far apart and move at random much faster, so a gas doesn't have a fixed shape and can flow. The density of a gas is much less than that of a solid or liquid.

> **2** *How is the arrangement of the particles in a gas different from that in a liquid?*

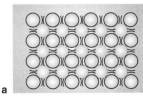 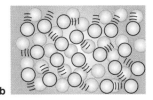 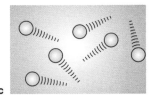

a          b          c

The arrangement of particles in **a** a solid, **b** a liquid and **c** a gas

**Key words:** solid, liquid, gas

## Key points

- Flow, shape, volume and density are the properties used to describe each state of matter.
- The particles in a solid are held next to each other, vibrating in their fixed positions.
- The particles in a liquid move about at random and are in contact with each other.
- The particles in a gas move about randomly and are much farther apart than particles in a solid or liquid.

### Bump up your grade

Make sure that you can describe the arrangement of the particles in each of the three states of matter.

---

Student Book
pages 30–31 **P1**

# 1.4 Conduction

- **Conduction** occurs mainly in solids. Most liquids and all gases are poor **conductors**.
- If one end of a solid is heated, the particles at that end gain kinetic energy and vibrate more. This energy is passed to neighbouring particles and in this way the energy is transferred through the solid.
- This process occurs in metals.
- In addition, when metals are heated their **free electrons** gain kinetic energy and move through the metal, transferring energy by colliding with other particles. Hence all metals are good conductors.

> **1** *Why are saucepans often made of metal with wooden handles?*

- Poor conductors are called **insulators**. Materials such as wool and fibreglass are good insulators because they contain trapped air.

> **2** *Why are materials that trap air good insulators?*

**Key words:** conduction, conductor, free electron, insulator

## Key points

- Metals are the best conductors.
- Materials such as wool and fibreglass are good insulators.
- Conduction in a metal is mainly due to free electrons transferring energy inside the metal.
- Non-metals are poor conductors because they do not contain free electrons.

### AQA Examiner's tip

Know some examples of insulators and how they are used.

Student Book
pages 32–33
**P1**

# 1.5 Convection

- **Convection** occurs in **fluids**. Fluids are liquids and gases.
- When a fluid is heated it expands. The fluid becomes less dense and rises. The warm fluid is replaced by cooler, denser fluid. The resulting **convection current** transfers energy throughout the fluid.

▐▶ **1** *Why doesn't convection occur in solids?*

- Convection currents can be on a very small scale, such as heating water in a beaker, or on a very large scale, such as heating the air above land and sea. Convection currents are responsible for onshore and offshore breezes.

▐▶ **2** *Why does a fluid become less dense when it is heated?*

**Bump up your grade**

Make sure that you can explain how convection currents are set up, in terms of the changes in density when a fluid is heated.

**Key words:** convection, fluid, convection current

---

Student Book
pages 34–35
**P1**

# 1.6 Evaporation and condensation

**Bump up your grade**

Make sure you know the factors that affect the rate of evaporation and condensation.

- **Evaporation** is when a liquid turns into a gas. Evaporation takes place because the most energetic liquid molecules escape from the liquid's surface and enter the air. Therefore, the average kinetic energy of the remaining molecules is less, so the **temperature** of the liquid decreases. This means that evaporation causes cooling.

- The rate of evaporation is increased by:
  - increasing the surface area of the liquid
  - increasing the temperature of the liquid
  - creating a draught of air across the liquid's surface.

▐▶ **1** *What effect would decreasing the surface area of a liquid have on its rate of evaporation?*

- **Condensation** is when a gas turns into a liquid. This often takes place on cold surfaces such as windows and mirrors.

- The rate of condensation is increased by:
  - increasing the surface area
  - reducing the surface temperature.

▐▶ **2** *What effect would decreasing the surface area of a liquid have on its rate of condensation?*

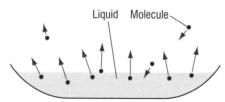

Water molecules escaping from a liquid

**Key words:** evaporation, temperature, condensation

# 1.7 Energy transfer by design

## Key points

- The rate of energy transfer to or from an object depends on:
  - the shape, size and type of material of the object
  - the materials the object is in contact with
  - the temperature difference between the object and its surroundings.

**Motorcycle engine fins**

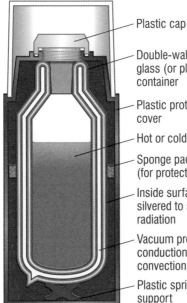

Plastic cap

Double-walled glass (or plastic) container

Plastic protective cover

Hot or cold liquid

Sponge pad (for protection)

Inside surfaces silvered to stop radiation

Vacuum prevents conduction and convection

Plastic spring for support

**A vacuum flask**

- The greater the **temperature difference** between an object and its surroundings, the greater the rate at which energy is transferred.
- The rate at which energy is transferred also depends on:
  - the materials the object is in contact with
  - the object's shape
  - the object's surface area.
- Sometimes we want to **maximise** the rate of energy transfer to keep things cool. To do this we may use things that:
  - are good conductors
  - are painted dull black
  - have the air flow around them maximised.

▸ **1** *Why does painting an object dull black maximise the rate of energy transfer?*

- Sometimes we want to **minimise** the rate of energy transfer to keep things warm. To do this we need to minimise the transfer of energy by conduction, convection and radiation. We may use things that:
  - are good insulators
  - are white and shiny
  - prevent convection currents by trapping air in small pockets.

▸ **2** *Why does trapping air in small pockets minimise the rate of energy transfer?*

### AQA Examiner's tip

Be prepared to apply your knowledge of energy transfer to different situations. These might include animal adaptations to hot or cold climates.

### Bump up your grade

A vacuum flask is an application that often comes up in examination questions. Make sure that you can relate the structure of a vacuum flask to minimising energy transfer by conduction, convection and radiation. A vacuum flask reduces the rate of energy transfer to keep hot things hot and cold things cold.

**Key words:** temperature difference, maximise, minimise

# 1.8 Specific heat capacity

- The greater the mass of an object, the more slowly its temperature increases when it is heated.

- The rate of temperature change in a substance when heated depends on the energy transferred to it, its mass and its specific heat capacity.

**AQA** *Examiner's tip*

Note that in the equation, $\theta$ is the temperature change. In an exam question it may be necessary to work out the change in temperature by subtracting the initial temperature from the final temperature.

- When we heat a substance, we transfer energy to it which will increase its temperature. The **specific heat capacity** of a substance is the amount of energy required to raise the temperature of 1 kilogram of the substance by 1 degree Celsius.

- Different substances have different specific heat capacities. The greater the specific heat capacity, the more energy required for each degree temperature change. For example, the specific heat capacity of aluminium is 900 J/kg°C and of copper is 490 J/kg°C. If we wanted to raise the temperature of 1 kg of aluminium, we would need to transfer almost twice the energy needed to raise the temperature of 1 kg of copper by the same amount.

  **1** *The specific heat capacity of oil is 2100 J/kg°C. How much energy is needed to raise the temperature of 1 kg of oil by 1°C?*

- The greater the **mass** of substance being heated the more energy required for each degree temperature change. If we had a 2 kg piece of copper, we would need to transfer twice the energy needed to raise the temperature of 1 kg of copper by the same amount.

  **2** *The specific heat capacity of water is 4200 J/kg°C. How much energy is needed to raise the temperature of 2 kg of water by 1°C?*

- The equation for specific heat capacity is: $E = m \times c \times \theta$
  Where:
  $E$ is energy transferred, J
  $m$ is mass, kg
  $c$ is specific heat capacity, J/kg°C
  $\theta$ is temperature change, °C.

**Key words:** specific heat capacity, mass

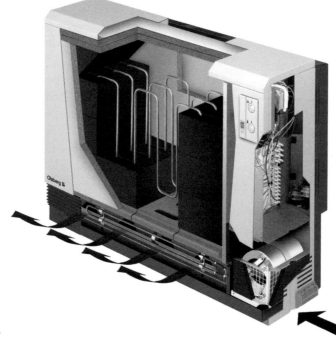

Storage heater

# 1.9 Heating and insulating buildings

## Key points

- The rate of energy transfer to or from our homes can be reduced.

- U-values tell us how much energy per second passes through different materials. The lower the U-value the better the material is as an insulator.

- Solar heating panels do not use fuel to heat water but they are expensive to buy and install.

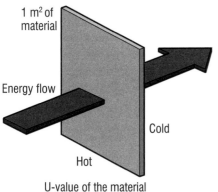

1 m² of material

Energy flow

Cold

Hot

U-value of the material
= energy/s passing per m²
for 1°C temperature difference

**U-values**

### Bump up your grade

Be prepared to look at tables of U-values and decide which would be the best material to use in a particular situation. You may also have to take into account other things such as cost-effectiveness and payback time.

### How Science Works

- Most people want to minimise the rate of **energy transfer** out of their homes to reduce fuel bills. This can be done by fitting:
  - fibreglass loft insulation to reduce energy transfer by conduction
  - cavity wall insulation that traps air in small pockets to reduce energy transfer by convection
  - double glazing to reduce energy transfer by conduction through windows
  - draught proofing to reduce energy transfer by convection
  - aluminium foil behind radiators to reflect infrared radiation back into the room.

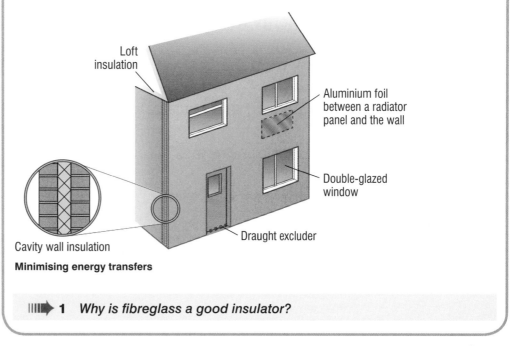

Loft insulation

Aluminium foil between a radiator panel and the wall

Double-glazed window

Draught excluder

Cavity wall insulation

**Minimising energy transfers**

▭▶ **1** *Why is fibreglass a good insulator?*

- The U-value of a material tells us how much energy per second passes through it. Knowing the U-values of different materials allows us to compare them. The lower the U-value the better the material is as an insulator.

- **Solar heating panels** contain water that is heated by radiation from the Sun. This water may then be used to heat buildings or provide domestic hot water. Solar heating panels are cheap to run because they do not use fuel. However, they are expensive to buy and install, and the water is not heated at night.

▭▶ **2** *Why are the pipes that contain the water in a solar heating panel often painted black?*

**Key words:** energy transfer, solar heating panel

**1** What is the best colour for a central heating radiator, glossy white or dull black?

**2** Why does a solid have a fixed volume?

**3** When a liquid evaporates, why is the average kinetic energy of the remaining molecules reduced?

**4** What happens to the rate of energy transfer between an object and its surroundings if the temperature difference between them is reduced?

**5** Which types of energy transfer involve particles?

**6** How does energy from the Sun reach the Earth?

**7** How does the colour of a surface affect the rate of conduction?

**8** Why are gases poor conductors?

**9** Why are metals the best conductors?

**10** What is convection?

**11** How does cavity wall insulation reduce energy transfer from a house?

**12** The specific heat capacity of water is 4200 J/kg °C. How much energy is needed to raise the temperature of 3 kg of water by 4°C?

| Chapter checklist | ✓ | ✓ | ✓ |
|---|---|---|---|
| **Tick when you have:** | | | |
| reviewed it after your lesson ✔ ☐ ☐ | | | |
| revised once – some questions right ✔ ✔ ☐ | | | |
| revised twice – all questions right ✔ ✔ ✔ | | | |
| *Move on to another topic when you have all three ticks* | | | |

| | ✓ | ✓ | ✓ |
|---|---|---|---|
| Infrared radiation | ☐ | ☐ | ☐ |
| Surfaces and radiation | ☐ | ☐ | ☐ |
| States of matter | ☐ | ☐ | ☐ |
| Conduction | ☐ | ☐ | ☐ |
| Convection | ☐ | ☐ | ☐ |
| Evaporation and condensation | ☐ | ☐ | ☐ |
| Energy transfer by design | ☐ | ☐ | ☐ |
| Specific heat capacity | ☐ | ☐ | ☐ |
| Heating and insulating buildings | ☐ | ☐ | ☐ |

Student Book
pages 44–45 **P1**

# 2.1 Forms of energy

- Energy exists in different forms.
- Energy can be transferred from one form into another form.
- When an object falls and gains speed, its gravitational potential energy decreases and its kinetic energy increases.

- Energy exists in different forms such as: light, sound, **kinetic** (movement), nuclear, **electrical**, **gravitational potential**, **elastic potential** and **chemical**.
- The last three are forms of stored energy.

> **1** *What form of energy does a compressed spring have?*

- Energy can be transferred from one form to another.
- Any object above the ground has gravitational potential energy.
- A falling object transfers gravitational potential energy to kinetic energy.

> **2** *Where does the chemical energy stored in your muscles come from?*

**Bump up your grade**

Make sure that you are familiar with the different forms that energy can take and know some examples of each of them.

**Key words:** kinetic energy, electrical energy, gravitational potential energy, elastic potential energy, chemical energy

Student Book
pages 46–47 **P1**

# 2.2 Conservation of energy

- Energy can be transferred from one form to another, or from one place to another.
- Energy cannot be created or destroyed.
- Conservation of energy applies to all energy changes.

- It is not possible to create or destroy energy. It is only possible to transfer it from one form to another, or from one place to another.
- This means that the total amount of energy is always the same. This is called the **conservation of energy** and it applies to all energy transfers.

> **1** *What energy transfers take place when you turn on a torch?*

- For example, when an object falls, gravitational potential energy is transferred to kinetic energy.
- Similarly, stretching an elastic band transfers chemical energy to elastic potential energy.
- In a solar cell, light energy is transferred to electrical energy.

> **2** *In terms of energy, what happens when you burn a fuel?*

- A swinging pendulum transfers energy from gravitational potential energy to kinetic energy and back again as it swings.

**AQA** *Examiner's tip*

Conservation of energy is an extremely important idea in physics, so it will often come up in examination questions.

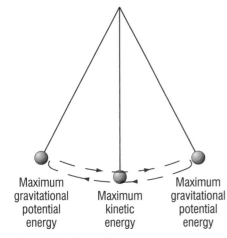

Maximum gravitational potential energy — Maximum kinetic energy — Maximum gravitational potential energy

**A pendulum in motion**

**Key words:** conservation of energy

# 2.3  Useful energy

- A **machine** is something that transfers energy from one place to another or from one form to another.
- The energy we get out of a machine consists of:
  - **useful energy**, which is transferred to the place we want and in the form we want it
  - **wasted energy**, which is not usefully transferred.

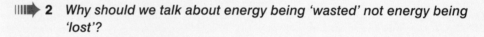

▐▐▐➡ **1**  *What happens to the wasted energy from a light bulb?*

- Both the useful energy and the wasted energy will eventually be transferred to the surroundings, and make them warm up. As the energy spreads out, it becomes more difficult to use for further energy transfers.
- Energy is often wasted because of friction between the moving parts of a machine. This energy warms the machine and the surroundings.
- Sometimes friction may be useful, for example in the brakes of a bicycle or a car. Some of the kinetic energy of the vehicle is transferred to energy heating the brakes.

▐▐▐➡ **2**  *Why should we talk about energy being 'wasted' not energy being 'lost'?*

### Key points

- Useful energy is energy in the place we want it and the form we need it.
- Wasted energy is energy that is not useful energy.
- Useful energy and wasted energy both end up being transferred to the surroundings, which become warmer.
- As energy spreads out, it gets more and more difficult to use for further energy transfers.

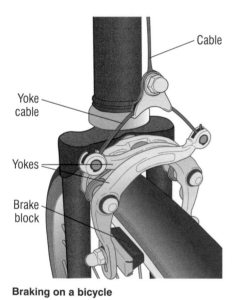

Cable

Yoke cable

Yokes

Brake block

**Braking on a bicycle**

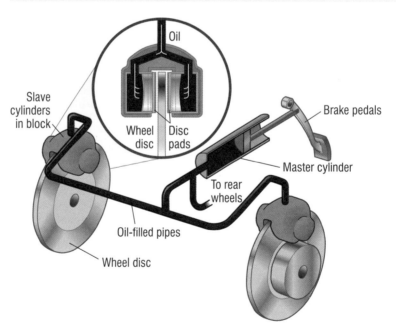

Oil

Slave cylinders in block

Wheel disc

Disc pads

Brake pedals

Master cylinder

To rear wheels

Oil-filled pipes

Wheel disc

**Disc brakes**

### Bump up your grade

Sometimes wasted energy is transferred as sound, but the amount of energy is usually very small. Remember that this energy will also eventually be transferred to the surroundings making them warmer.

**Key words:** machine, useful energy, wasted energy

# 2.4 Energy and efficiency

● Energy is measured in **joules (J)**. This unit is used for all forms of energy.

● The energy supplied to a machine is often called the **input energy**. From the conservation of energy we know that:

input energy (energy supplied) = useful energy transferred + energy wasted

● The less energy that is wasted by a machine, the more efficient the machine.

● We can calculate the **efficiency** of any appliance that transfers energy, using the equation:

$$\text{Efficiency} = \frac{\text{useful energy transferred by the appliance}}{\text{total energy supplied to the appliance}} \ (\times \ 100\%)$$

## Key points

● The efficiency of an appliance = useful energy transferred by the appliance ÷ total energy supplied to the appliance (×100%).

● No machine can be more than 100% efficient.

● Measures to make machines more efficient include reducing:
  – friction
  – air resistance
  – electrical resistance
  – noise due to vibrations.

⮕ **1** *In a light bulb, for every 25 joules of energy that are supplied to the bulb, 5 joules are usefully transferred into light energy. What is the efficiency of the bul*

● The efficiency can be ...... multiplied by 100 to give a percentage.

● No appliance can ...... an electric heater, which usefully transfers all of ...... it by heating its surroundings.

⮕ **2** ...... stes less energy because of friction. Wr...... of the machine?

● The energy tran...... ppliance can be represented with a **Sankey diagram**.

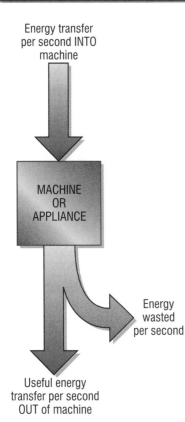

Energy transfer
per second INTO
machine

MACHINE
OR
APPLIANCE

Energy
wasted
per second

Useful energy
transfer per second
OUT of machine

**A Sankey diagram**

**AQA** **Examiner's tip**

Remember that no appliance can be more than 100% efficient. So if you do an efficiency calculation and the answer is greater than 1 (or 100%), you have made an error and should check your working.

**Bump up your grade**

Efficiency is a ratio. That means it does not have a unit.

**Key words:** joule (J), input energy, efficiency, Sankey diagram

**1** What form of energy does a moving car have?

**2** What form of energy does a stretched spring have?

**3** When is electrical energy transferred?

**4** What are the useful energy transfers that take place in a hairdryer?

**5** What are the useful energy transfers that take place in a television?

**6** What energy transfers take place when you lift a ball into the air and then drop it so it falls to the ground?

**7** Wear and tear causes a particular machine to waste more energy. What happens to the efficiency of this machine?

**8** In an electric motor, 250 J of energy are transferred to the surroundings by heating, for every 1000 J of electrical energy supplied. What is the efficiency of the motor as a fraction?

**9** Why is an electric heater the only appliance that may have an efficiency of 1, or 100%?

**10** Why do electrical appliances such as televisions and computers have vents?

**11** 60 J of energy are supplied each second to a light bulb. The bulb transfers 18 J of energy to light each second. How much energy does the bulb waste each second?

**12** When a kettle full of cold water is brought to boiling point, 720 000 J of energy are transferred to the water. If the kettle has an efficiency of 96%, how much energy is supplied to the kettle to boil the water?

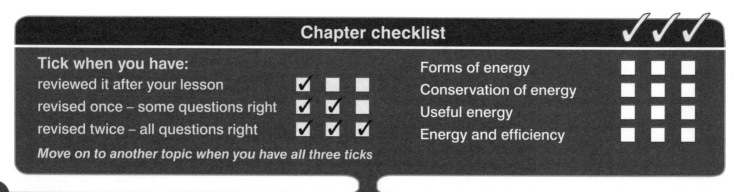

**Chapter checklist** ✓ ✓ ✓

Tick when you have:

| | | | | | | | |
|---|---|---|---|---|---|---|---|
| reviewed it after your lesson | ✓ | ☐ | ☐ | Forms of energy | ☐ | ☐ | ☐ |
| revised once – some questions right | ✓ | ✓ | ☐ | Conservation of energy | ☐ | ☐ | ☐ |
| revised twice – all questions right | ✓ | ✓ | ✓ | Useful energy | ☐ | ☐ | ☐ |
| | | | | Energy and efficiency | ☐ | ☐ | ☐ |

*Move on to another topic when you have all three ticks*

Student Book
pages 54–55 **P1**

# 3.1 Electrical appliances

### Key points

- Electrical appliances can transfer electrical energy into useful energy at the flick of a switch.

- Uses of everyday electrical appliances include heating, lighting, making objects move and creating sound and visual images.

- An electrical appliance is designed for a particular purpose and should waste as little energy as possible.

- **Electrical appliances** are extremely useful. They transfer electrical energy into whatever form of energy we need at the flick of a switch.
- Common electrical appliances include:
  - lamps, to produce light
  - electric mixers, to produce kinetic energy
  - speakers, to produce sound energy
  - televisions, to produce light and sound energy.

▶ 1 *What useful energy transfer takes place in an electric drill?*

- Many electrical appliances transfer energy by heating. This may be a useful transfer, for example in a kettle, but energy is often wasted. Appliances should be designed to waste as little energy as possible.

▶ 2 *Which electrical appliance usefully transfers electrical energy into light energy and sound energy?*

**Key word:** electrical appliance

---

Student Book
pages 56–57 **P1**

# 3.2 Electrical power

### Key points

- Power is rate of transfer of energy.

- $P = \dfrac{E}{t}$

- Efficiency = $\dfrac{\text{useful power out}}{\text{total power in}}$ (×100%)

**Rocket power**

- The **power** of an appliance is the rate at which it transfers energy.
- The unit of power is the **watt**, symbol W. An appliance with a power of 1 watt transfers 1 joule of electrical energy to other forms of energy every second.
- Often a watt is too small a unit to be useful, so power may be given in **kilowatts (kW)**. 1 kilowatt = 1000 watts.

▶ 1 *How many watts are equivalent to 12 kilowatts?*

- Power is given by the equation: $P = \dfrac{E}{t}$
  Where:
  $P$ is the power in watts, W
  $E$ is the energy in joules, J
  $t$ is the time taken (in seconds) for the energy to be transferred.
- Power is the energy per second transferred or supplied, so we can write the efficiency equation in terms of power:

$$\text{Efficiency} = \frac{\text{useful power out}}{\text{total power in}} \ (\times 100\%)$$

▶ 2 *An electric motor transfers 48 kJ of electrical energy into kinetic energy in 2 minutes. What is the useful power output of the motor?*

**Bump up your grade**

Be sure that you practise efficiency calculations using both fractions and percentages.

**Key words:** power, watt, kilowatt (kW)

Student Book
pages 58–59

**P1**

# 3.3 Using electrical energy

## Key points

- The kilowatt-hour is the energy supplied to a 1 kW appliance in 1 hour.
- $E = P \times t$
- Total cost = number of kWh × cost per kWh.

An electricity meter

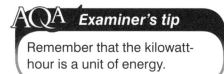

**Examiner's tip**

Remember that the kilowatt-hour is a unit of energy.

- Companies that supply mains electricity charge customers for the amount of electrical energy used. Because of the large numbers involved, the joule is not a suitable unit. The amount of energy used is measured in **kilowatt-hour (kWh)**.

- A kilowatt-hour is the amount of energy that is transferred by a one-kilowatt appliance when used for one hour.

- The amount of energy transferred to a mains appliance can be found using the equation:  $E = P \times t$

Where:
$E$ is the energy transferred in kilowatt-hours, kWh
$P$ is the power of the appliance in kW
$t$ is the time taken (in hours) for the energy to be transferred.

> **1** *How much electrical energy, in kWh, is transferred when a 9 kW shower is used for 15 minutes?*

- The electricity meter in a house records the number of kWh of energy used. If the previous meter reading is subtracted from the current reading, the electrical energy used between the readings can be calculated.

An electricity meter will record the energy usage of all appliances in use

- The cost of the electrical energy supplied is found using the equation:

**total cost = number of kWh × cost per kWh**

- The cost per kWh is given on the electricity bill.

> **2** *The price of 1 kWh of electrical energy is 9p. How much does it cost to use a 60 W electric light for 4 hours?*

**Key word:** kilowatt-hour (kWh)

# 3.4 Cost effectiveness matters

## Key points

- Cost effectiveness means getting the best value for money.
- To compare the cost effectiveness of different appliances, we need to take account of a number of different costs.

### AQA Examiner's tip

In the examination you may be given data on different appliances and asked to compare the data to decide which appliance is the most cost effective.

- To compare the **cost effectiveness** of different appliances we must consider a number of different costs.
- These may include:
  - the cost of buying the appliance
  - the cost of installing the appliance
  - the running costs
  - the maintenance costs
  - environmental costs
  - the interest charged on a loan to buy the appliance.

⏵ **1** *What might environmental costs include?*

- Many householders want to reduce their energy bills. To do this they may buy newer, more efficient appliances (such as a new fridge). They could also install materials designed to reduce energy wastage (such as loft insulation).
- The **payback time** is the time it takes for an appliance or installation to pay for itself in terms of energy savings.

⏵ **2** *Loft insulation costs £600 including installation. It saves £80 per year on the fuel bill. How long is the payback time?*

### Bump up your grade

Make sure that you can work out the payback time for different appliances or methods of insulation.

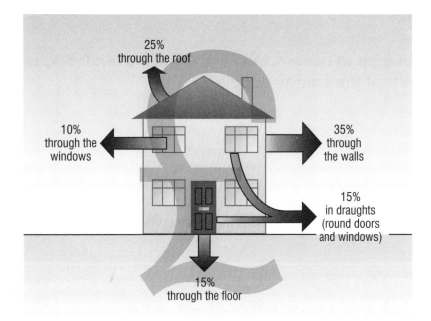

25%
through the roof

10%
through the
windows

35%
through
the walls

15%
in draughts
(round doors
and windows)

15%
through the floor

**Energy loss from a house**

**Key words:** cost effectiveness, payback time

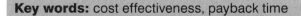

**1** What is the useful energy transfer in an electric toaster?

**2** How may energy be wasted in an electric heater?

**3** How may energy be wasted in an electric kettle?

**4** How many kilowatts are equivalent to 30 000 watts?

**5** Which is more powerful, a 2000 W hairdryer or a 2.2 kW hairdryer?

**6** What quantity is measured in kilojoules?

**7** An electric light bulb transfers 6000 J of energy in 1 minute. What is its power?

**8** How much electrical energy, in kW h, is transferred when a 2 kW iron is used for 30 minutes?

**9** Why is the electrical energy supplied by the mains measured in kilowatt-hours?

**10** A machine has an input power rating of 100 kW and a useful output power of 40 kW. What is its percentage efficiency?

**11** Electricity costs 12p per kW h. What is the cost of using a 2.5 kW h heater for 2 hours?

**12** It costs 6.6p to use a 1.2 kW microwave oven for 30 minutes. What is the cost per kW h of the energy supplied?

[H]

| Chapter checklist | ✓ | ✓ | ✓ |
|---|---|---|---|
| **Tick when you have:** | | | |
| reviewed it after your lesson | ✓ | ☐ | ☐ |
| revised once – some questions right | ✓ | ✓ | ☐ |
| revised twice – all questions right | ✓ | ✓ | ✓ |
| *Move on to another topic when you have all three ticks* | | | |

| | | | |
|---|---|---|---|
| Electrical appliances | ☐ | ☐ | ☐ |
| Electrical power | ☐ | ☐ | ☐ |
| Using electrical energy | ☐ | ☐ | ☐ |
| Cost effectiveness matters | ☐ | ☐ | ☐ |

# 4.1 Fuel for electricity

- Electricity generators in power stations are driven by turbines.

- Coal, oil and natural gas are burned in fossil-fuel power stations.

- Uranium or plutonium is used as the fuel in a nuclear power station.

- Biofuels are renewable sources of energy which can generate electricity.

### Bump up your grade

Most power stations burn fuels to produce energy to heat water. In a nuclear power station uranium is not burned; the energy comes from the process of nuclear fission.

- In most power stations, water is heated to produce steam. The steam drives a **turbine**, which is coupled to an electrical **generator** that produces the electricity.

- The energy can come from burning a **fossil fuel** such as coal, oil or gas. Fossil fuels are obtained from long-dead biological material.

- In some gas-fired power stations, hot gases may drive the turbine directly. A gas-fired turbine may be switched on very quickly.

- A **biofuel** is any fuel obtained from living or recently living organisms. Some biofuels can be used in small-scale, gas-fired power stations. Biofuels are renewable sources of energy.

**1** *Name three fossil fuels.*

- In a nuclear power station, the fuel used is uranium (or sometimes plutonium).

- The nucleus of a uranium atom can undergo a process called **nuclear fission**. This process releases energy.

- There are lots of uranium nuclei, so lots of fission reactions take place, releasing lots of energy. This energy is used to heat water, turning it into steam.

**2** *What is the process by which energy is produced in a nuclear power station?*

### How Science Works

- Much more energy is released per kilogram of uranium undergoing fission reactions than from each kilogram of fossil fuel that we burn.

- Nuclear power stations do not release any greenhouse gases, unlike fossil-fuel power stations. However, nuclear power stations do produce radioactive waste that must be safely stored for a long period of time.

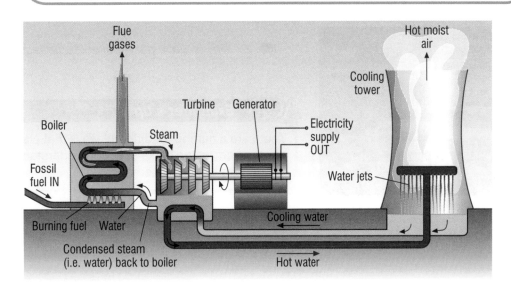

Inside a fossil fuel power station

**Key words:** turbine, generator, fossil fuel, biofuel, nuclear fission

# 4.2 Energy from wind and water

Energy from wind, waves and tides is called **renewable energy**. That's because these sources of energy can never be used up, unlike fossil fuels or nuclear fuels.

**Key points**

- A wind turbine is an electricity generator on top of a tall tower.
- Waves generate electricity by turning a floating generator.
- Hydroelectricity generators are turned by water running downhill.
- A tidal power station traps each high tide and uses it to turn generators.

## Wind

- We can use energy from **wind** and water to drive turbines directly.
- In a wind turbine, the wind passing over the blades makes them rotate and drive a generator at the top of a narrow tower.

## Water

- Electricity can be produced from energy obtained from **falling water**, **waves** or **tides**.
- **Hydroelectric power.** At a hydroelectric power station, water is collected in a reservoir. This water is allowed to flow downhill and turn turbines at the bottom of the hill.
- In a pumped storage system, surplus electricity is used, at times of low demand, to pump the water back up the hill to the top reservoir. This means that the energy is stored. Then at times of high demand the water can be released to fall through the turbines and transfer the stored energy to electrical energy.

> **1** *What form of energy is stored in the water in the top reservoir of a pumped storage scheme?*

**A wind farm**

- **Wave power.** We can use the movement of the waves on the sea to generate electricity. The movement drives a floating turbine that turns a generator. Then the electricity is delivered to the grid system on shore by a cable.
- **Tidal power.** The level of the sea around the coastline rises and falls twice each day. These changes in sea level are called tides. If a barrage is built across a river estuary, the water at each high tide can be trapped behind it. When the water is released to fall down to the lower sea level, it drives turbines.

> **2** *Why is wave power likely to be less reliable than tidal power?*

**AQA** *Examiner's tip*

There are a number of different ways that electricity can be generated using energy from water. Make sure you understand them and can describe the differences between them.

**A tidal power station**

**Key words:** renewable energy, wave, tide

# 4.3 Power from the Sun and the Earth

- Solar cells transfer solar energy directly into electricity.
- Solar heating panels use the Sun's energy to heat water directly.
- Geothermal energy comes from inside the Earth.

**Bump up your grade**

Know some examples of where solar energy is particularly useful for producing electricity.

- **Solar energy** from the Sun travels through space to the Earth as electromagnetic radiation.
- A **solar cell** can transfer this energy into electrical energy. Each cell only produces a small amount of electricity, so they are useful to power small devices such as watches and calculators.
- We can also join together large numbers of the cells to form a solar panel.
- Water flowing through a **solar heating panel** is heated directly by energy from the Sun.
- A **solar power tower** uses thousands of mirrors to reflect sunlight onto a water tank to heat the water and produce steam.

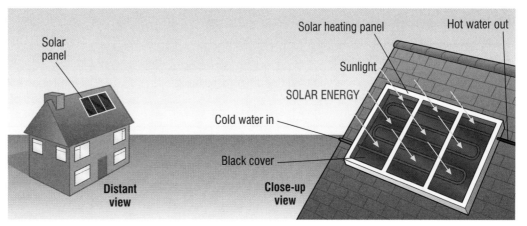

Solar water heating

**1** Why are large numbers of solar cells often joined to make a solar panel?

- **Geothermal energy** is produced inside the Earth by radioactive processes and this heats the surrounding rock. In volcanic or other suitable areas, very deep holes are drilled and cold water is pumped down to the hot rocks. There it is heated and comes back to the surface as steam. The steam is used to drive turbines that turn generators and so electricity is produced.
- In a few parts of the world, hot water comes up to the surface naturally and can be used to heat buildings nearby.

**2** Why are only a few places in the world able to have geothermal power stations?

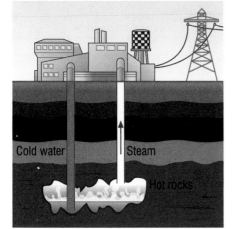

A geothermal power station

**Key words:** solar energy, solar cell, solar power tower, geothermal energy

# 4.4 Energy and the environment

- Coal, oil, gas and uranium are **non-renewable** energy resources. The rate at which they are being used up is very much faster than the rate at which they are produced.
- Oil and gas will probably run out in the next fifty years or so, although coal will last much longer.
- **Renewable** energy resources will not run out. They can be produced as fast as they are used.
- Scientists are investigating ways to reduce the environmental impact of using fossil fuels. For example sulfur may be removed from fuel before burning. Instead of allowing carbon dioxide to be released into the atmosphere from power stations, it could be captured and stored in old oil and gas fields.
- There are advantages and disadvantages to using each type of energy resource.

| Energy resource | Advantages | Disadvantages |
|---|---|---|
| **Coal** | Bigger reserves than the other fossil fuels<br>Reliable | Non-renewable<br>Production of $CO_2$, a greenhouse gas<br>Production of $SO_2$, causing acid rain |
| **Oil** | Reliable | Non-renewable<br>Production of $CO_2$, a greenhouse gas<br>Production of $SO_2$, causing acid rain |
| **Gas** | Reliable | Non-renewable<br>Production of $CO_2$, a greenhouse gas |
| **Nuclear** | No production of polluting gases<br>Reliable | Non-renewable<br>Produces hazardous nuclear waste, which is difficult to dispose of safely<br>Small risk of a big nuclear accident |
| **Wind** | Renewable<br>No production of polluting gases<br>Free energy resource | Requires many large turbines<br>Not reliable, as the wind does not always blow |
| **Falling water** | Renewable<br>No production of polluting gases<br>Reliable in wet areas<br>Free energy resource | Only works in wet and hilly areas<br>Damming the areas causes flooding and affects the local ecology |
| **Waves** | Renewable<br>No production of polluting gases<br>Free energy resource | Can be a hazard to boats<br>Not reliable |
| **Tides** | Renewable<br>No production of polluting gases<br>Reliable, always tides twice a day<br>Free energy resource | Only a few river estuaries are suitable<br>Building a barrage affects the local ecology |
| **Solar** | Renewable<br>No production of polluting gases<br>Reliable in hot countries, in the daytime<br>Free energy resource | Solar cells only produce a small amount of electricity<br>Unreliable in less sunny countries |
| **Geothermal** | Renewable<br>No production of polluting gases<br>Free energy resource | Only economically viable in a very few places<br>Drilling through large depth of rock is difficult and expensive |

⫸ **1** *What type of area would be most suitable for a wind farm?*

⫸ **2** *What is the difference between a renewable energy resource and a non-renewable energy resource?*

⫸ **3** *Which gas, released by the burning of coal, causes acid rain?*

**Key word:** non-renewable

---

Student Book
pages 72–73  **P1**

## 4.5  The National Grid

### Key points

- The National Grid distributes electricity from power stations to our homes.
- Step-up and step-down transformers are used in the National Grid.
- A high grid voltage reduces energy wastage and makes the system more efficient.

**Bump up your grade**

Remember that step-up transformers increase the voltage and step-down transformers decrease the voltage.

- In Britain, electricity is distributed through the **National Grid**. This is a network of pylons and cables that connects power stations to homes, schools, factories and other buildings. Since the whole country is connected to the system, power stations can be switched in or out of the grid according to demand.

- The cables are carried long distances across the countryside supported by overhead pylons. In towns and close to homes the cables are buried underground.

⫸ **1** *Give two advantages of overhead cables compared to underground cables.*

- The National Grid's voltage is 132 000 V or more. Power stations produce electricity at a voltage of 25 000 V.

- In power stations, electricity is generated at a particular voltage. The voltage is increased by **step-up transformers** before the electricity is transmitted across the National Grid. This is because transmission at high voltage reduces the energy wasted in the cables, making the system more efficient.

- It would be dangerous to supply electricity to consumers at these very high voltages. So, at local substations, **step-down transformers** are used to reduce the voltage to 230 V for use in homes and offices.

⫸ **2** *What sort of transformers are used at local substations?*

**AQA** **Examiner's tip**

You do not need to remember the voltage of the power stations or the National Grid. But you need to know that the mains voltage in homes is 230 V.

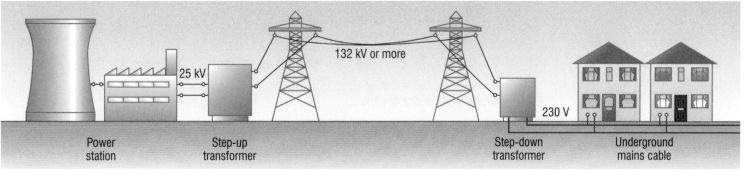

25 kV     132 kV or more     230 V

Power station    Step-up transformer    Step-down transformer    Underground mains cable

**The National Grid**

**Key words:** National Grid, step-up transformer, step-down transformer

## 4.6 Big energy issues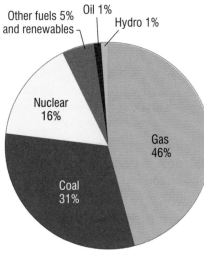

### Key points

- Gas-fired power stations and pumped-storage stations can meet variations in demand.

- Nuclear, coal and oil power stations can meet base-load demand.

- Nuclear power stations, fossil-fuel power stations using carbon capture and renewable energy are all likely to contribute to future energy supplies.

- A constant amount of electricity is provided by nuclear, coal-fired and oil-fired power stations. This is called the **base load** demand.

- The demand for electricity varies during the day and between summer and winter.

> **1** *Why does the demand for electricity vary between summer and winter?*

- This variable demand is met using gas-fired power stations, pumped-storage schemes and renewable energy sources.

- When demand is low, energy is stored by pumping water to the top reservoir of pumped storage schemes.

- Different types of power station have different **start-up times**. Gas-fired power stations have the shortest start-up times and nuclear power stations have the longest.

> **2** *In what form is energy stored in the top reservoir of a pumped storage scheme?*

**AQA** *Examiner's tip*

You may be asked to argue for or against a particular type of power station in an exam question. If data on the power station is provided in the question, make sure that you use it in your answer.

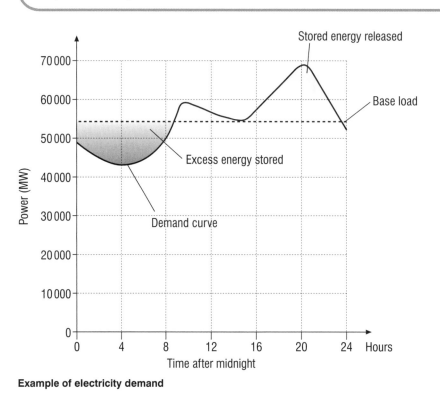

Example of electricity demand

**Energy sources for electricity**

---

**Key words:** base load, start-up time

1. Give three examples of biofuels.

2. Why do hydroelectric power stations have to be built in hilly areas?

3. Give three situations in which energy can be obtained from water to produce electricity.

4. What is a fossil fuel?

5. Where does geothermal energy come from?

6. Give two examples of where solar energy is particularly useful for producing electricity.

7. What is a solar cell?

8. What is a solar heating panel?

9. Are renewable or non-renewable energy sources the most reliable?

10. What are the disadvantages of using fossil fuels in power stations to produce electricity?

11. What colour are the pipes in a solar heating panel usually painted?

12. State three advantages of geothermal energy.

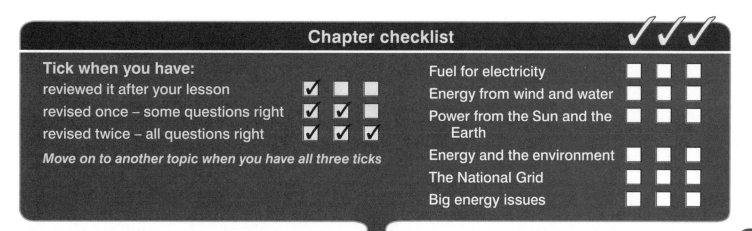

**Chapter checklist** ✓ ✓ ✓

**Tick when you have:**

reviewed it after your lesson ✓ ☐ ☐

revised once – some questions right ✓ ✓ ☐

revised twice – all questions right ✓ ✓ ✓

*Move on to another topic when you have all three ticks*

| | | | |
|---|---|---|---|
| Fuel for electricity | ☐ | ☐ | ☐ |
| Energy from wind and water | ☐ | ☐ | ☐ |
| Power from the Sun and the Earth | ☐ | ☐ | ☐ |
| Energy and the environment | ☐ | ☐ | ☐ |
| The National Grid | ☐ | ☐ | ☐ |
| Big energy issues | ☐ | ☐ | ☐ |

# 5.1 The nature of waves

- We use waves to transfer energy and information. The direction of travel of the wave is the direction in which the wave transfers energy.
- There are different types of wave:
- For a **transverse wave** the **oscillation** (vibration) of the particles is **perpendicular** (at right angles) to the direction in which the wave travels.

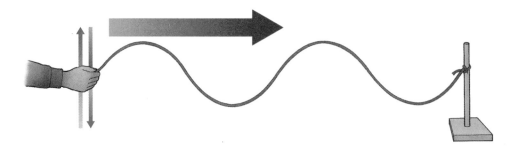

Transverse waves

- For a **longitudinal wave** the oscillation of the particles is parallel to the direction of travel of the wave.
- A longitudinal wave is made up of **compressions** and **rarefactions**.

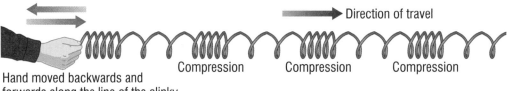

Direction of travel

Compression    Compression    Compression

Hand moved backwards and
forwards along the line of the slinky

Longitudinal waves on a slinky

> **1** *When a longitudinal wave passes through air, what happens to the air particles at a compression?*

- **Electromagnetic waves**, e.g. light waves and radio waves, can travel through a vacuum. There are no particles moving in an electromagnet wave, as these waves are oscillations in electric and magnetic fields. The oscillations are perpendicular to the direction of travel of the wave. So all electromagnetic waves are transverse waves.
- **Mechanical waves**, e.g. waves on springs, and sound waves, travel through a medium (substance). Mechanical waves may be transverse or longitudinal.
- Sound waves are longitudinal waves.

> **2** *What type of wave can be produced on a stretched string?*

**Key words:** transverse wave, oscillation, perpendicular, longitudinal wave, compression, rarefaction, electromagnetic wave, mechanical wave

## Key points

- We use waves to transfer energy and to transfer information.
- Transverse waves vibrate at right angles to the direction of energy transfer. All electromagnetic waves are transverse waves.
- Longitudinal waves vibrate parallel to the direction of energy transfer. A sound wave is a longitudinal wave.
- Mechanical waves, which need a medium (substance) to travel through, may be transverse or longitudinal waves.

**AQA** *Examiner's tip*

If you are asked to show what is meant by longitudinal and transverse waves, you may find it easier to draw labelled diagrams than to give descriptions in words.

# 5.2 Measuring waves

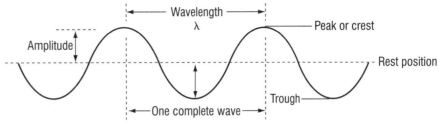

A transverse wave

## Key points

- For any wave, its amplitude is the height of the wave crest or the depth of the wave trough, from the position at rest.

- For any wave, its frequency is the number of wave crests passing a point in one second.

- For any wave, its wavelength is the distance from one wave crest to the next wave crest. This is the same as the distance from one wave trough to the next wave trough.

- $v = f \times \lambda$

### Bump up your grade

Make sure that you know what the wave terms mean and can mark them on a diagram.

- The **amplitude** of a wave is the height of the wave crest or the depth of the wave trough from the position at rest.

- The greater the amplitude of a wave the more energy it carries.

- The **wavelength** of a wave is the distance from one crest to the next crest, or from one trough to the next trough.

- The **frequency** of a wave is the number of wave crests passing a point in one second. The unit of frequency is the hertz (Hz). This unit is equivalent to per second (s).

- The **speed** of a wave is given by the equation: $v = f \times \lambda$

  Where:
  $v$ is the wave speed in metres per second, m/s
  $f$ is the frequency in hertz, Hz
  $\lambda$ is the wavelength in metres, m.

> **1** *What is the speed of waves with a frequency of 5 Hz and a wavelength of 2 m?*

- The diagram shows a transverse wave, but the same terms apply to a longitudinal wave.

- The wavelength of a longitudinal wave is the distance from the middle of one compression to the middle of the next compression. This is the same as the middle of one rarefaction to the middle of the next rarefaction.

- The frequency of a longitudinal wave is the number of compressions passing a point in one second.

> **2** *What is the unit of frequency?*

**Key words:** amplitude, wavelength, frequency, speed

# 5.3 Wave properties: reflection

- The image seen in a mirror is due to the **reflection** of light.

- The diagram shows how an image is formed by a **plane** (flat) **mirror**. The incident ray is the ray that goes towards the mirror. The reflected ray is the one coming away from the mirror.

- We draw a line, called the **normal**, perpendicular to the mirror at the point where the incident ray hits the mirror.

- The **angle of incidence** is the angle between the incident ray and the normal.

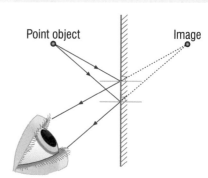

Incident ray from a ray box

$\hat{i} = \hat{r}$  Normal

*i*

*r*

Reflected ray

Mirror

**The law of reflection**

- The **angle of reflection** is the angle between the reflected ray and the normal.

- For any reflected ray the angle of incidence is equal to the angle of reflection.

▐▶ **1** *What is the normal?*

- The image in a plane mirror is:
  - the same size as the object
  - upright
  - the same distance behind the mirror as the object is in front.
  - virtual.

- A **real image** is one that can be formed on a screen, because the rays of light that produce the image actually pass through it.

- A **virtual image** cannot be formed on a screen, because the rays of light that produce the image only appear to pass through it.

Point object

Image

**Image formation by a plane mirror**

▐▶ **2** *What size is the image in a plane mirror?*

**Key words:** plane mirror, normal, angle of incidence, angle of reflection, real image, virtual image

# 5.4 Wave properties: refraction

## Key points

- Refraction of light is the change of direction of a light ray when it crosses a boundary between two transparent substances.

- If the speed is reduced, refraction is towards the normal (e.g. air to glass).

- If the speed is increased, refraction is away from the normal (e.g. glass into air).

- Waves change speed when they cross a **boundary** between different substances. The wavelength of the waves also changes, but the frequency stays the same.

- **Refraction** is a property of all waves, including light and sound. For example, a light ray refracts when it crosses a boundary between two substances such as air and glass, or air and water.

- The change in speed of the waves causes a change in direction.

- When light enters a more dense substance, such as going from air to glass, it slows down and the ray changes direction towards the normal.

- When light enters a less dense substance, such as going from glass to air, it speeds up and the ray changes direction away from the normal.

- However, if the wave is travelling along a normal, then it will not change direction.

**Refraction by a prism**

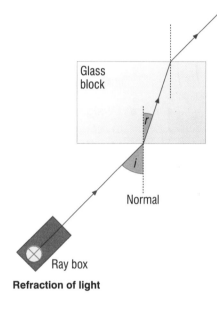

**Refraction of light**

▏▏▶ **1  Why does refraction take place?**

- Different colours of light have different wavelengths, and are refracted by slightly different amounts. When a ray of white light is shone onto a triangular glass prism we can see this because a spectrum is produced. This is called dispersion.

- Violet light is refracted the most.

- Red light is refracted the least.

▏▏▶ **2  Why does light split up into different colours when it passes through a triangular prism?**

## AQA  *Examiner's tip*

Take care not to confuse reflection and refraction.

## ▲ *Bump up your grade*

Remember that a ray of light travelling along a normal is **not** refracted.

**Key words:** boundary, refraction

Student Book
pages 86–87

**P1**

# 5.5 Wave properties: diffraction

## Key points

- Diffraction is the spreading out of waves when they pass through a gap or round the edge of an obstacle.

- The narrower a gap the greater the diffraction.

- If radio waves do not diffract enough when they go over hills, radio and TV reception will be poor.

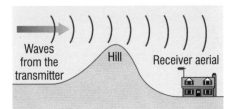

**Poor reception**

- **Diffraction** is a property of all waves, including light and sound. It is the spreading of waves when they pass through a gap or round an obstacle.

- The effect is most noticeable if the wavelength of the waves is about the same size as the gap or the obstacle.

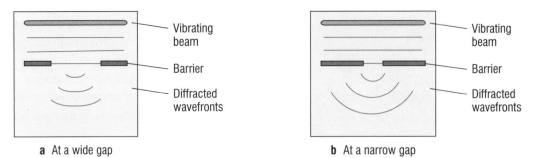

**a** At a wide gap  **b** At a narrow gap

**Diffraction of waves by a gap: a** a wide gap **b** a narrow gap

▶ **1** *Why don't we often observe the diffraction of light during everyday life?*

- TV signals are carried by radio waves. People living in hilly areas may not be able to receive a signal because it is blocked by a hill. Radio waves passing the hill will be diffracted round the hill. If they do not diffract enough, the radio and TV signals will be poor.

▶ **2** *What sort of waves are diffracted?*

**Bump up your grade**

If you are drawing a diagram to show diffraction, make sure that the wavelength of the waves stays the same.

**Key word:** diffraction

---

Student Book
pages 88–89

**P1**

# 5.6 Sound

## Key points

- The frequency range of the normal human ear is from about 20 Hz to about 20 kHz.

- Sound waves are longitudinal.

- Sound waves need a medium in which to travel.

- Reflections of sound are called echoes.

- **Sound** is caused by mechanical vibrations in a substance, and travels as a wave.

- It can travel through liquids, solids and gases. Sound waves generally travel fastest in solids and slowest in gases.

- They cannot travel through a vacuum (like space). This can be tested by listening to a ringing bell in a 'bell jar'. As the air is pumped out of the jar, the ringing sound fades away.

- Sound waves are longitudinal waves. The direction of the vibrations is the same as the direction in which the wave travels.

- The range of frequencies that can be heard by the human ear is from 20 Hz to 20 000 Hz. The ability to hear the higher frequencies declines with age.

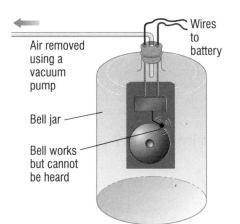

Air removed using a vacuum pump

Wires to battery

Bell jar

Bell works but cannot be heard

**A sound test**

- Sound waves can be reflected to produce **echoes**:
  - Only hard, flat surfaces such as flat walls and floors reflect sound.
  - Soft things like carpets, curtains and furniture absorb sounds.
  - An empty room will sound different once carpets, curtains and furniture are put into it.
- Sound waves can be refracted. Refraction takes place at the boundaries between layers of air at different temperatures.
- Sound waves can also be diffracted.

> **1** *What is the range of frequencies that can be heard by the human ear?*
> **2** *What is the reflection of a sound called?*

**Key words:** sound, echo

---

Student Book pages 90–91 **P1**

# 5.7 Musical sounds

## Key points

- The pitch of a note increases if the frequency of the sound waves increases.
- The loudness of a note depends on the amplitude of the sound waves.
- Vibrations created in an instrument when it is played produce sound waves.

**a** Loud and high-pitched

**b** Loud and low-pitched

**c** Quiet and high-pitched (higher pitch than **a**)

**Different sounds**

**Tuning fork waves as they appear on an oscilloscope**

- The **pitch** of a note depends on the frequency of the sound waves. The higher the frequency of the wave, the higher the pitch of the sound.
- The loudness of a sound depends on the amplitude of the sound waves. The greater the amplitude the more energy the wave carries and the louder the sound.
- Differences in **waveform** can be shown on an oscilloscope.

> **1** *What happens to the pitch of a note as the frequency decreases?*

- Tuning forks and signal generators produce 'pure' waveforms.
- The quality of a note depends on the waveform.
- Different instruments produce different waveforms, which is why they sound different from each other.
- Vibrations created in an instrument when it is played produce sound waves.
- In some instruments (e.g. a saxophone) a column of air vibrates. In others (e.g. a violin) a string vibrates. Some instruments vibrate when they are struck, e.g. a xylophone.

> **2** *Why do different instruments sound different when they play the same note?*

### Bump up your grade

Practise sketching waveforms, e.g. sketch a wave with twice the frequency and half the amplitude of the original.

**Key word:** pitch

**1** What is the unit of wavelength?

**2** What type of image is produced by a plane mirror?

**3** If you stand 1.5 m in front of a plane mirror, where will your image be?

**4** Which colour of light is refracted the most?

**5** What is an echo?

**6** What is a rarefaction?

**7** What happens when light waves cross a boundary between two transparent substances?

**8** What is diffraction?

**9** How does a flute produce sound?

**10** What does the pitch of a note depend on?

**11** What is the speed of a sound wave of frequency 330 Hz and wavelength 1 cm?

**12** What is the frequency of a wave if it travels at 400 m/s and its wavelength is 20 m?

[H]

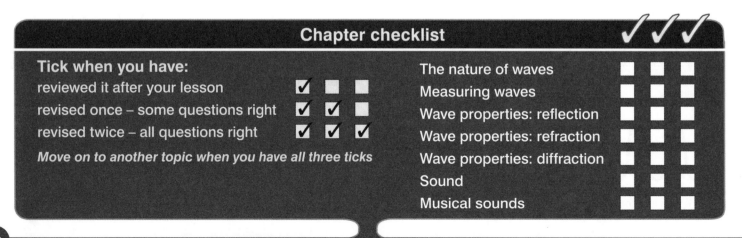

**Chapter checklist** ✔ ✔ ✔

**Tick when you have:**

reviewed it after your lesson ✔ ☐ ☐

revised once – some questions right ✔ ✔ ☐

revised twice – all questions right ✔ ✔ ✔

*Move on to another topic when you have all three ticks*

| | ✔ | ✔ | ✔ |
|---|---|---|---|
| The nature of waves | ☐ | ☐ | ☐ |
| Measuring waves | ☐ | ☐ | ☐ |
| Wave properties: reflection | ☐ | ☐ | ☐ |
| Wave properties: refraction | ☐ | ☐ | ☐ |
| Wave properties: diffraction | ☐ | ☐ | ☐ |
| Sound | ☐ | ☐ | ☐ |
| Musical sounds | ☐ | ☐ | ☐ |

Student Book
pages 94–95

**P1**

# 6.1 The electromagnetic spectrum

- Electromagnetic radiations are electric and magnetic disturbances. They travel as waves and move energy from place to place.
- All electromagnetic waves travel through space (a vacuum) at the same speed but they have different wavelengths and frequencies.
- All of the waves together are called the **electromagnetic spectrum**. We group the waves according to their **wavelength** and **frequency**:
  - Gamma rays have the shortest wavelength and highest frequency.
  - Gamma rays can have wavelengths as short as $10^{-15}$ m (= 0.000 000 000 000 001 m).
  - Radio waves have the longest wavelength and lowest frequency.
  - Radio waves can have wavelengths of more than 10 000 m.
- The spectrum is continuous. The frequencies and wavelengths at the boundaries are approximate as the different parts of the spectrum are not precisely defined.
- Different wavelengths of electromagnetic radiation are reflected, absorbed or transmitted differently by different substances and types of surface.
- The higher the frequency of an electromagnetic wave the more energy it transfers.

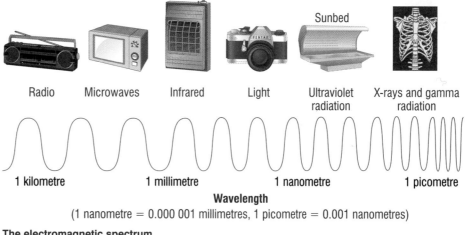

| Radio | Microwaves | Infrared | Light | Ultraviolet radiation | X-rays and gamma radiation |

1 kilometre    1 millimetre    1 nanometre    1 picometre

**Wavelength**

(1 nanometre = 0.000 001 millimetres, 1 picometre = 0.001 nanometres)

**The electromagnetic spectrum**

- All electromagnetic waves travel through space at a **wave speed** of 300 million m/s. We can link the speed of the waves to their wavelength and frequency using the equation:

$$v = f \times \lambda$$

Where:
$v$ is the wave speed = 300 000 000 m/s
$f$ is the frequency in hertz, Hz
$\lambda$ is the wavelength in metres, m.

> 1 **What is the unit of frequency?**
> 2 **Which part of the electromagnetic spectrum transfers the most energy?**

**Key words:** gamma ray, X-ray, ultraviolet radiation, electromagnetic spectrum, wave speed

Student Book
pages 96–97

**P1**

# 6.2 Light, infrared, microwaves and radio waves

### Key points

- White light contains all the colours of the spectrum.
- Visible light, infrared radiation, microwaves and radio waves are all used for communication.

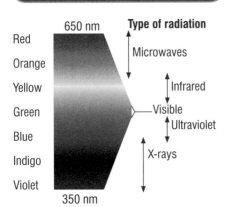

**Parts of the electromagnetic spectrum**

- **Visible light** is the part of the electromagnetic spectrum that is detected by our eyes. We see the different wavelengths within it as different colours.
- The wavelength increases across the spectrum from violet to red. We see a mixture of all the colours as white light.
- Visible light can be used for photography.
- Infrared (IR) radiation is given out by all objects. The hotter the object, the more IR it emits. Remote controls for devices such as TVs and CD players use IR.
- **Microwaves** are used in communications. Microwave transmitters produce wavelengths that are able to pass through the atmosphere. They are used to send signals to and from satellites and within mobile phone networks.
- **Radio waves** transmit radio and TV programs and carry mobile phone signals.

▷ **1** *Which have the longer wavelengths, microwaves or radio waves?*

- Microwave radiation and radio waves penetrate your skin and are absorbed by body tissue. This can heat internal organs and may damage them.
- Infrared radiation is absorbed by skin; too much will burn your skin.

**Key words:** visible light, microwave, radio wave

---

Student Book
pages 98–99

**P1**

# 6.3 Communications

### Key points

- Radio waves of different frequencies are used for different purposes.
- Microwaves are used for satellite TV signals.
- Research is needed to evaluate whether or not mobile phones are safe to use.
- Optical fibres are very thin fibres that are used to transmit signals by light and infrared radiation.

An optical fibre

- An alternating voltage applied to an aerial emits radio waves with the same frequency as the alternating voltage. When the waves are received they produce an alternating current in the aerial with the same frequency as the radiation received.
- The radio and microwave spectrum is divided into different **bands**. The different bands are used for different communications purposes.
- The shorter the wavelength of the waves the more information they carry, the shorter their range, the less they spread out.

▷ **1** *How are radio waves produced?*

- Mobile phones communicate with a local mobile phone mast using wavelengths just on the border between radio waves and microwaves. They are usually referred to as microwaves.
- Some scientists think that the radiation from mobile phones may affect the brain, especially in children.
- **Optical fibres** are very thin glass fibres. We use them to transmit signals carried by **visible light** or **infrared radiation**. The signals travel down the fibre by repeated total internal reflection.
- Optical fibres carrying visible light or infrared are useful in communications because they carry much more information and are more secure than radio wave and microwave transmissions.

**Key words:** band, optical fibre

# 6.4 The expanding universe

- Light from distant galaxies is red-shifted.
- Red-shift provides evidence that the universe is expanding.

**AQA** *Examiner's tip*

Remember that light is shifted towards the red end of the spectrum; it is **not** turned into red light.

- Imagine a wave source is moving relative to an observer. The wavelength and frequency of the waves detected by the observer will have changed (shifted) from the original produced by the source. This is called the **Doppler effect**.

- When the source moves away from the observer, the observed wavelength increases and the frequency decreases.

- When the source moves towards the observer, the observed wavelength decreases and the frequency increases.

- The Doppler effect can be demonstrated with sound waves. For example, an ambulance siren will sound different depending on whether it is moving away from you (pitch is lower) or towards you (pitch is higher).

▐▐▐▶ **1** *What happens to the wavelength if a wave source is moving away from you?*

- Galaxies are large collections of stars. Light observed from distant galaxies has been 'shifted' towards the red end of the spectrum. This is known as **red-shift** and means that the frequency has decreased and the wavelength increased.

- A **blue-shift** would indicate that a galaxy is moving towards us. We are able to see these effects by observing dark lines in the spectra from galaxies.

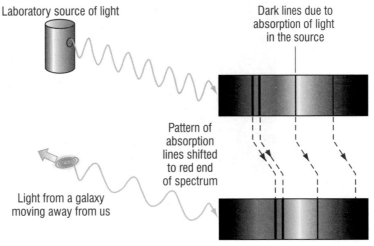

Laboratory source of light

Dark lines due to absorption of light in the source

Pattern of absorption lines shifted to red end of spectrum

Light from a galaxy moving away from us

**Red-shift**

- The further away the galaxy, the bigger the red-shift. This suggests that distant galaxies are moving away from us, and the most distant galaxies are moving the fastest. This is true of galaxies no matter which direction you look.

- All the distant galaxies are moving away from each other, so the whole universe is expanding.

▐▐▐▶ **2** *Which galaxies are moving fastest?*
▐▐▐▶ **3** *How does red-shift show that the universe is expanding?*

**Key words:** Doppler effect, red-shift, blue-shift

Student Book
pages 102–103

**P1**

# 6.5 The Big Bang

- Red-shift gives us evidence that the universe is expanding outwards in all directions.

- We can imagine going back in time to see where the universe came from. If it is now expanding outwards, this suggests that it started with a massive explosion at a very small initial point. This is known as the **Big Bang theory**.

▸ **1** *What is the Big Bang theory?*

The Big Bang

- If the universe began with a Big Bang, then high energy gamma radiation would have been produced. As the universe expanded, this would have become lower-energy radiation.

- Scientists discovered microwaves coming from every direction in space. This is **cosmic microwave background radiation** (CMBR), the radiation produced by the Big Bang.

- The Big Bang theory is so far the only way to explain the existence of CMBR.

▸ **2** *What happens to the wavelength of radiation as it changes from gamma to microwave?*

### Bump up your grade

Be sure that you can explain why red-shift is evidence for an expanding universe and the Big Bang.

## Key points

- The universe started with the Big Bang; a massive explosion from a very small initial point.

- The universe has been expanding ever since the Big Bang.

- Cosmic microwave background radiation (CMBR) is electromagnetic radiation created just after the Big Bang.

- At present CMBR can only be explained by the Big Bang theory.

**Key words:** Big Bang theory, cosmic microwave background radiation

**1** Which part of the electromagnetic spectrum has the longest wavelengths?

**2** Which part of the electromagnetic spectrum is between X-rays and visible light?

**3** The wave speed for all electromagnetic waves is 300 million m/s. What is the frequency of electromagnetic waves with a wavelength of 300 m?

**4** Which part of the electromagnetic spectrum transfers the least energy?

**5** Which part of the electromagnetic spectrum is used to transmit signals to and from satellites?

**6** How does visible light travel along an optical fibre?

**7** What is the Doppler effect?

**8** What is a galaxy?

**9** What has happened to the frequency of light that reaches Earth from distant galaxies?

**10** How can we tell if light from a distant galaxy has been red-shifted?

**11** What has happened to the gamma radiation produced at the time of the Big Bang?

**12** What piece of evidence can only be explained by the Big Bang theory?

| Chapter checklist | ✓ ✓ ✓ |
|---|---|

| Tick when you have: | | | | | | | |
|---|---|---|---|---|---|---|---|
| reviewed it after your lesson | ✓ | | | The electromagnetic spectrum | ☐ | ☐ | ☐ |
| revised once – some questions right | ✓ | ✓ | | Light, infrared, microwaves and radio waves | ☐ | ☐ | ☐ |
| revised twice – all questions right | ✓ | ✓ | ✓ | Communications | ☐ | ☐ | ☐ |
| *Move on to another topic when you have all three ticks* | | | | The expanding universe | ☐ | ☐ | ☐ |
| | | | | The Big Bang | ☐ | ☐ | ☐ |

1 An electric kettle is used to heat water. When the kettle is switched on, the energy is transferred to the water by a heating element at the bottom of the kettle.

    a    State the process that transfers energy from the heating element to the water at the bottom of the kettle. *(1 mark)*

    b    Eventually all of the water in the kettle becomes hot. Explain how energy is transferred from the water at the bottom of the kettle to the rest of the water. *(4 marks)*

    c    The kettle contains 1.2 kg of water. The temperature of the water is increased by 80 °C. Calculate the energy supplied to the water by the heating element. The specific heat capacity of the water is 4200 J/kg °C.
Write down the equation you use. Show clearly how you work out your answer and give the unit. *(3 marks)*

    d    Not all of the energy supplied to the kettle is transferred to the water. Explain what happens to the energy not transferred to the water. *(3 marks)*

2 *In this question you will be assessed on using good English, organising information clearly and using specialist terms where appropriate.*
There are three states of matter: solid, liquid and gas. The kinetic theory of matter tells us that solids, liquids and gases consist of particles. Use the kinetic theory to describe and explain the properties of solids, liquids and gases. *(6 marks)*

3 A food processor contains an electric motor.

    a  i    What is the useful energy transfer that takes place in the motor? *(1 mark)*
       ii    How is some energy wasted in the motor? *(1 mark)*

    b  i    The motor wastes 300 J of energy for every 1000 J of energy supplied to it. How much useful energy is transferred? *(1 mark)*
       ii    Calculate the percentage efficiency of the motor.
Write down the equation you use. Show clearly how you work out your answer and give the unit. *(3 marks)*

    c    The power of the motor is 800 W. If electricity costs 12p per kW h, calculate the cost of using the food processor for 15 minutes. *(4 marks)*

4 Energy can be produced using renewable and non-renewable energy sources. In a nuclear power station, energy is produced from uranium by nuclear fission.

    a    Is uranium a renewable or a non-renewable energy source? *(1 mark)*

    b    Explain how the energy from nuclear fission is used to generate electricity. *(4 marks)*

    c    Wind turbines use a renewable energy source to produce electricity.
       i    Explain the advantages of using a nuclear power station, compared to using a wind turbine, to generate electricity. *(2 marks)*
       ii    Explain the disadvantages of using a nuclear power station, compared to using a wind turbine, to generate electricity. *(2 marks)*

AQA **Examiner's tip**

**Qu 1b** There are four marks for explaining how the energy is transferred, so to get four marks make sure you make four points.

AQA **Examiner's tip**

**Qu 3bii** Be careful with percentages – this question has asked for the answer to be converted to a percentage, so you must multiply your answer by 100.

**5** A student is investigating the reflection of light. He stands a plane mirror on a piece of paper and marks the position of the back of the mirror with a line.

**a** Why should he mark the position of the back of the mirror? *(1 mark)*

**b** He pushes a pin into the paper in front of the mirror. The image of the pin in the mirror is virtual.

   i Explain what is meant by a virtual image. *(2 marks)*

   ii The pin is 6 cm from the line and 4 cm tall. Describe the image of the pin. *(3 marks)*

**c** The diagram shows the positions of the mirror and the pin.

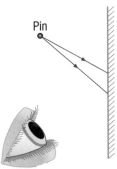

Pin

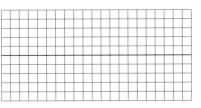

Copy and complete the diagram to show how the virtual image is formed. *(3 marks)*

**6** A teacher uses a tuning fork to produce a note.

**a** Describe how a sound wave from the tuning fork travels through the air. *(3 marks)*

**b** The teacher uses a microphone and an oscilloscope to produce a trace of the note from the tuning fork. The trace is shown below.

   i Copy and complete the diagram below to show what the trace would look like for a note that had the same pitch as the original note, but was louder. *(3 marks)*

   ii Copy and complete the diagram below to show what the trace would look like for a note that had the same volume as the original note, but a higher pitch. *(3 marks)*

AQA **Examiner's tip**

Make sure that you use a sharp pencil and ruler to complete the diagram as neatly as you can. Add arrows to show the direction of the rays and use dashed lines to represent virtual rays.

**Motion**

# 1.1 Distance–time graphs

- We can use graphs to help us describe the motion of an object.
- A distance–time graph shows the distance of an object from a starting point (y-axis) against time taken (x-axis).
- The **speed** of an object is the distance travelled each second.
- The gradient of the line on a distance–time graph represents speed. The steeper the gradient, the greater the speed.
- If an object is stationary, the line on a distance–time graph is horizontal.
- If an object is moving at a constant speed, the line on a distance–time graph is a straight line that slopes upwards.

▐▐▐▶ **1** *What is the SI unit of distance?*

- We can calculate the speed of an object using the equation:

$$\text{Speed in metres per second, m/s} = \frac{\text{distance travelled in metres, m}}{\text{time taken in seconds, s}}$$

▐▐▐▶ **2** *What is the speed of a runner who covers 400 m in 50 s?*

**Key word:** speed

### Key points

- The gradient of the line on a distance–time graph represents an object's speed.
- The steeper the line on a distance–time graph, the greater the speed it represents.
- Speed (m/s) = $\dfrac{\text{distance travelled (m)}}{\text{time taken (s)}}$

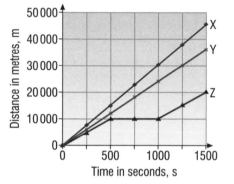

**Comparing distance–time graphs**

# 1.2 Velocity and acceleration

- The **velocity** of an object is its speed in a given direction.
- If the object changes direction it changes velocity, even if its speed stays the same.
- If the velocity of an object changes, we say that it accelerates.

▐▐▐▶ **1** *What is the difference between speed and velocity?*

- We can calculate **acceleration** using the equation:

$$a = \frac{v - u}{t}$$

Where:
a is the acceleration in metres per second squared, m/s²
v is the final velocity in metres per second, m/s
u is the initial velocity in metres per second, m/s
t is the time taken for the change in seconds, s.

▐▐▐▶ **2** *What is the SI unit of acceleration?*

- If the value calculated for acceleration is negative, the body is decelerating – slowing down. A **deceleration** is the same as a **negative acceleration**.

**Key words:** velocity, acceleration, deceleration

### Key points

- Velocity is speed in a given direction.
- Acceleration is the change of velocity per second.

$$a = \frac{v - u}{t}$$

⚠ **Bump up your grade**

Be sure to learn the units here carefully. Don't confuse m/s (unit of speed and velocity) and m/s² (unit of acceleration).

Student Book
pages 112–113   **P2**

# 1.3 More about velocity–time graphs

- A velocity–time graph shows the velocity of an object (*y*-axis) against time taken (*x*-axis).
- The gradient of the line on a velocity–time graph represents acceleration.
- The steeper the gradient, the greater the acceleration.
- If the line on a velocity–time graph is a horizontal, the acceleration is zero. Therefore the object is travelling at a steady speed.
- If the gradient of the line is negative, the object is decelerating.

## Key points

- If the line on a velocity–time graph is horizontal, the acceleration is zero.
- The gradient of a velocity–time graph represents acceleration.
- The area under the line on a velocity–time graph is the distance travelled.   **[H]**

The **area** under the line on a velocity–time graph represents the distance travelled in a given time. The bigger the area, the greater the distance travelled.

*Higher*

> **1** What does a horizontal line on a velocity–time graph represent?
> **2** What would the velocity–time graph for a steadily decelerating object look like?

---

Student Book
pages 114–115   **P2**

# 1.4 Using graphs

*Higher*

## Key points

- The speed of an object is given by the gradient of the line on its distance–time graph.   **[H]**
- The acceleration of an object is given by the gradient of the line on its velocity–time graph.   **[H]**
- The distance travelled by an object is given by the area under the line of its velocity–time graph.   **[H]**

**AQA** *Examiner's tip*

Take care not to confuse distance–time graphs and velocity–time graphs.

> **1** What does an upwardly curving line represent on a:
> **a** distance–time graph
> **b** velocity–time graph?

### Using distance–time and velocity–time graphs

If you calculate the gradient of the line on a distance–time graph for an object, your answer will be the speed of the object.

If you calculate the gradient of the line on a velocity–time graph for an object, your answer will be the acceleration of the object.

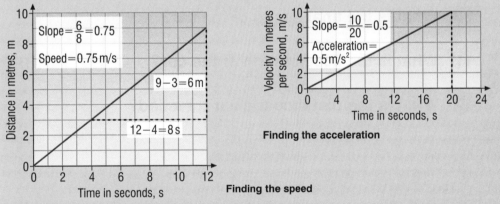

Slope $= \frac{6}{8} = 0.75$

Speed $= 0.75\,\text{m/s}$

$9 - 3 = 6\,\text{m}$

$12 - 4 = 8\,\text{s}$

**Finding the speed**

Slope $= \frac{10}{20} = 0.5$

Acceleration $= 0.5\,\text{m/s}^2$

**Finding the acceleration**

Calculating the area under the line between two times on a velocity–time graph gives the distance travelled between those times.

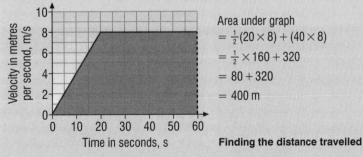

Area under graph
$= \frac{1}{2}(20 \times 8) + (40 \times 8)$
$= \frac{1}{2} \times 160 + 320$
$= 80 + 320$
$= 400\,\text{m}$

**Finding the distance travelled**

Always use the numbers from the graph scales in any calculations.

**1** What is the average speed, in m/s, of a car that completes a distance of 1.2 km in 1 minute?

**2** What does the distance–time graph for a stationary object look like?

**3** What quantity has the unit m/s$^2$?

**4** What does a negative value for acceleration mean?

**5** What happens to the gradient of the line on a distance–time graph if the speed increases?

**6** How can an object travelling at a steady speed be accelerating?

**7** A car accelerates from rest to a speed of 40 m/s in 10 s. What is its acceleration?

**8** What part of a velocity–time graph represents distance travelled?

The graph shows the motion of a car.

**9** What is the initial speed of the car?

**10** What is the final speed of the car?

**11** What is the acceleration of the car?

[H]

**12** What is the distance the car travelled?

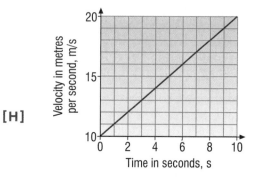

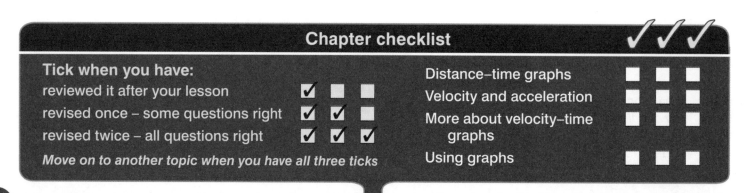

Student Book
pages 118–119 **P2**

# 2.1 Forces between objects

## Key points

- A force can change the shape of an object or change its motion or state of rest.
- The unit of force is the newton (N).
- When two objects interact they always exert equal and opposite forces on each other.

Direction of car

Force of tyre on road    Force of road on tyre

**Driving force**

**Key words:** force, newton

- **Forces** are measured in **newtons**, abbreviated to N.
- Objects always exert **equal** and **opposite** forces on each other. If object A exerts a force on object B, object B exerts an equal and opposite force on object A. These are sometimes called 'action and reaction' forces.

⟩⟩⟩ **1**  *What is the SI unit of force?*

- If a car hits a barrier, it exerts a force on the barrier. The barrier exerts a force on the car that is equal in size and in the opposite direction.
- If you place a book on a table, the weight of the book will act vertically downwards on the table. The table will exert an equal and opposite reaction force upwards on the book.
- When a car is being driven forwards there is a force from the tyre on the ground pushing backwards. There is an equal and opposite force from the ground on the tyre which pushes the car forwards.

⟩⟩⟩ **2**  *In what direction does the force of weight always act?*

AQA **Examiner's tip**

It is important to understand that action and reaction forces act on different objects. Remember that forces have both size and direction.

---

Student Book
pages 120–121 **P2**

# 2.2 Resultant force

## Key points

- The resultant force is a single force that has the same effect as all the forces acting on an object.
- If an object is accelerating there must be a resultant force acting on it.

### Bump up your grade

If an object is accelerating it can be speeding up, slowing down or changing direction.

**Key word:** resultant force

- Most objects have more than one force acting on them. The **resultant force** is the single force that would have the same effect on the object as all the original forces acting together.
- When the resultant force on an object is zero:
  - if the object is at rest, it will stay at rest
  - if the object is moving, it will carry on moving at the same speed and in the same direction.

⟩⟩⟩ **1**  *What is the unit of resultant force?*

- When the resultant force on an object is not zero, there will be an acceleration in the direction of the force.
- This means that:
  - If the object is at rest, it will accelerate in the direction of the resultant force.
  - If the object is moving in the same direction as the resultant force, it will accelerate in that direction.
  - If the object is moving in the opposite direction to the resultant force, it will decelerate.

⟩⟩⟩ **2**  *What is the resultant force of a 4 N force and a 3 N force acting in the same direction?*

# P2

# 2.3 Force and acceleration

- The bigger the resultant force on an object, the greater its acceleration.
- The greater the mass of an object, the smaller its acceleration for a given force.
- $F = m \times a$

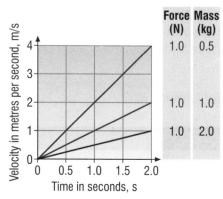

| Force (N) | Mass (kg) |
| --- | --- |
| 1.0 | 0.5 |
| 1.0 | 1.0 |
| 1.0 | 2.0 |

**Velocity–time graph for different combinations of force and mass**

- A **resultant force** always causes an **acceleration**. Remember that a deceleration is a negative acceleration. If there is no acceleration in a particular situation, the resultant force must be zero.
- Acceleration is a change in velocity. An object can accelerate by changing its direction even if it is going at a constant speed. So a resultant force is needed to make an object change direction.
- We can find the resultant force on an object using the equation:

$$F = m \times a$$

Where:
$F$ is the resultant force in newtons, N
$m$ is the mass in kilograms, kg
$a$ is the acceleration in m/s$^2$.

- The greater the resultant force on an object, the greater its acceleration. The bigger the **mass** of an object, the bigger the force needed to give it a particular acceleration.

> 1 *What happens to the acceleration of an object as the resultant force on it decreases?*
>
> 2 *What is the resultant force on a car of mass 1000 kg if its acceleration is 2 m/s$^2$?*

**Key word:** mass

# P2

# 2.4 On the road

- Friction and air resistance oppose the driving force of a car.
- The stopping distance of a car depends on the thinking distance and the braking distance.

### Bump up your grade

Remember that the reaction time depends on the driver. The braking distance depends on the road, weather conditions and the condition of the vehicle.

- If a vehicle is travelling at a steady speed, the resultant force on it is zero. The driving forces are equal and opposite to the frictional forces.

> 1 *What is the resultant force on a car travelling at a steady speed on a straight horizontal road?*

- The faster the speed of a vehicle, the bigger the deceleration needed to stop it in a particular distance. So the bigger the braking force needed.
- The **stopping distance** of a vehicle is the distance it travels during the driver's reaction time (the thinking distance) plus the distance it travels under the braking force (the braking distance).
- The **thinking distance** is increased if the driver is tired or under the influence of alcohol or drugs.
- The **braking distance** can be increased by:
  - poorly maintained roads or bad weather conditions
  - the condition of the car. For example, worn tyres or worn brakes will increase braking distance.

> 2 *What is the relationship between stopping distance, thinking distance and braking distance?*

**Key words:** stopping distance, thinking distance, braking distance

Student Book
pages 126–127 **P2**

# 2.5 Falling objects

## Key points

- The weight of an object is the force of gravity on it. Its mass is the quantity of matter in it.

- An object acted on only by gravity accelerates at about 10 m/s².

- The terminal velocity of a falling object is the velocity it reaches when it is falling in a fluid. The weight is then equal to the drag force on the object.

### Bump up your grade

Do not confuse mass and weight. Mass is the amount of matter in an object, and weight is the force of gravity acting on it.

### AQA Examiner's tip

The drag force may also be called air resistance or fluid resistance.

- If an object falls freely, the resultant force acting on it is the force of gravity. It will make an object close to the Earth's surface accelerate at about 10 m/s².
- We call the force of gravity **weight**, and the acceleration the **acceleration due to gravity**.
- The equation:

$$F = m \times a$$

Where:
$F$ is the resultant force in newtons, N
$m$ is the mass in kilograms, kg
$a$ is the acceleration in m/s²
becomes:

$$W = m \times g$$

Where:
$W$ is the weight in newtons, N
$m$ is the mass in kilograms, kg
$g$ is the acceleration due to gravity in m/s².

- If the object is on the Earth, not falling, $g$ is called the **gravitational field strength** and its units are newtons per kilogram, N/kg.
- When an object falls through a fluid, the fluid exerts a **drag force** on the object, resisting its motion. The faster the object falls, the bigger the drag force becomes, until eventually it will be equal to the weight of the object. The resultant force is now zero, so the body stops accelerating. It moves at a constant velocity called the **terminal velocity**.

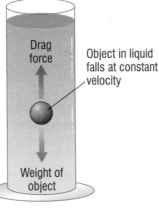

Drag force

Object in liquid falls at constant velocity

Weight of object

**Falling in a liquid**

▶ **1** Why does an object dropped in a fluid initially accelerate?
▶ **2** What eventually happens to an object falling in a fluid?

**Key words:** weight, gravitational field strength, drag force, terminal velocity

# 2.6 Stretching and squashing

## Key points

- The extension is the difference between the length of the spring and its original length.

- The extension of a spring is directly proportional to the force applied to it, provided the limit of proportionality is not exceeded.

- The spring constant of a spring is the force per unit extension needed to stretch it.

### AQA Examiner's tip

Two quantities are directly proportional to each other only if plotting them on a graph gives a straight line through the origin.

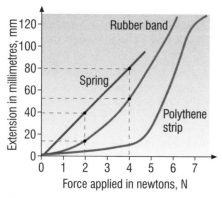

**Extension versus force applied for different materials**

- If we hang small weights from a spring it will stretch. The increase in length from the original is called the **extension**. When we remove the weights the spring will return to its original length.

- Objects and materials that behave in this way are called **elastic**.

- An elastic object is one that regains its original shape when the forces deforming it are removed.

▷ **1** *What is an inelastic object?*

- If we plot a graph of extension against force applied for a spring, we obtain a straight line that passes though the origin. This tells us that the extension is **directly proportional** to the force applied. If we apply too big a force, the line begins to curve because we have exceeded the **limit of proportionality**.

## Hooke's law

- Objects and materials that behave like this are said to obey **Hooke's law**. This states that the extension is directly proportional to the force applied, provided the limit of proportionality is not exceeded.

- We can write Hooke's law as an equation:

$$F = k \times e$$

Where:
$F$ is the force applied in newtons, N
$k$ is the **spring constant** of the spring in newtons per metre, N/m
$e$ is the extension in metres, m.

- The stiffer a spring is, the greater its spring constant.

- When an elastic object is stretched, work is done. This is stored as elastic potential energy in the object.

- When the stretching force is removed, this stored energy is released.

▷ **2** *A spring has a spring constant of 30 N/m. If the extension is 0.30 m, what is the force applied?*

▷ **3** *How can we tell when a spring has exceeded its limit of proportionality?*

**Key words:** elastic, directly proportional, limit of proportionality, Hooke's law

# 2.7 Force and speed issues

- Fuel economy of road vehicles can be improved by reducing the speed or fitting a wind deflector.

- Average speed cameras are linked in pairs and they measure the average speed of a vehicle.

- Anti-skid surfaces increase the friction between a car tyre and the road surface. This reduces skids, or even prevents skids altogether.

- Reducing the speed of a vehicle reduces the amount of fuel it uses to travel a particular distance. This is called fuel economy.

- Reducing the air resistance by making the vehicle more streamlined (e.g. fitting a wind deflector) also improves fuel economy.

- Speed cameras are used to discourage motorists from speeding. They can determine the speed of a motorist at a particular point. They can also be used in pairs to determine the speed at two points and so calculate an average speed. Motorists caught travelling above the speed limit are fined and may lose their driving licence.

- Skidding happens when the brakes on a vehicle are applied too harshly. When a vehicle skids the wheels lock and slide along the road surface, increasing the stopping distance.

- Anti-skid surfaces are used to reduce or prevent skidding. They are rougher than normal road surfaces, increasing the friction between the vehicle tyres and the road. They are used in places where drivers are likely to brake, such as near traffic lights and road junctions.

> **1** *Why does making a vehicle more streamlined improve fuel economy?*
> **2** *When a vehicle is travelling along a straight road at a steady speed what can you say about the engine force and the air resistance?*

**A speed camera**

**1** If you push on a wall with a horizontal force of 15 N to the right, what force will the wall exert on you?

**2** What happens to an object moving at a steady speed if the resultant force on it is zero?

**3** When will a resultant force cause a deceleration?

**4** What happens to the acceleration of an object as the resultant force on it increases?

**5** What is the resultant force on a car of mass 1500 kg if its acceleration is 0.5 m/s$^2$?

**6** What is the acceleration of a car of mass 2000 kg if the resultant force acting in its direction of motion is 800 N?

**7** What is the effect of the speed of a vehicle on its stopping distance?

**8** What is terminal velocity?

**9** What is the weight of a person of mass 70 kg?

**10** What is an elastic object?

**11** What does Hooke's law state?

**12** When a force of 10 N is applied to a spring it extends by 2.0 cm. What is the spring constant of the spring?

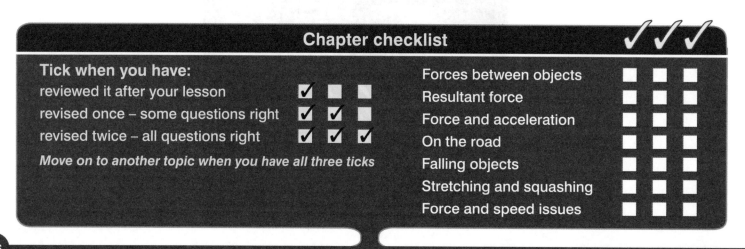

Chapter checklist

**Tick when you have:**
reviewed it after your lesson
revised once – some questions right
revised twice – all questions right

*Move on to another topic when you have all three ticks*

Forces between objects
Resultant force
Force and acceleration
On the road
Falling objects
Stretching and squashing
Force and speed issues

Student Book
pages 134–135

**P2**

# 3.1 Energy and work

## Key points

- Work is done on an object when a force makes the object move.
- Energy transferred = work done
- $W = F \times d$
- Work done to overcome friction is transferred as energy that heats the objects that rub together and the surroundings.

**Key words:** work, friction

- Whenever an object starts to move, a force must have been applied to it.
- When a force moves an object, energy is transferred and **work** is done.
- When work is done moving the object, the supplied energy is transferred to the object so the work done is equal to the energy transferred.
- Both work and energy have the unit joule, J.
- The work done on an object is calculated using the equation:

$$W = F \times d$$

Where:
$W$ is the work done in joules, J
$F$ is the force in newtons, N
$d$ is the distance moved in the direction of the force in metres, m.
Note that if the distance moved is zero, no work is done on the object.

- Work done to overcome **friction** is mainly transferred into energy by heating. When the brakes are applied to a vehicle, friction between the brake pads and the wheel discs opposes the motion of the wheel. The kinetic energy of the vehicle is transferred into energy that heats the brake pads and the wheel discs as well as the surrounding air.

> **1** *What is the SI unit of work done?*
> **2** *What is the work done on an object if a force of 300 N moves it a distance of 8 m?*

Student Book
pages 136–137

**P2**

# 3.2 Gravitational potential energy

## Key points

- The gravitational potential energy of an object depends on its weight and how far it moves vertically.
- $E_p = m \times g \times h$

### AQA Examiner's tip

Remember that the gravitational potential energy an object has is relative to another point, usually to the surface of the Earth. So we calculate changes in gravitational potential energy when an object is moved between two points.

**Key words:** gravitational potential energy, power

- **Gravitational potential energy** is energy stored in an object because of its position in the Earth's gravitational field. Whenever an object is moved vertically upwards it gains gravitational potential energy equal to the work done on it by the lifting force.
- The change in gravitational potential energy can be calculated using the equation:

$$E_p = m \times g \times h$$

Where:
$E_p$ is the change in gravitational potential energy in joules, J
$m$ is the mass in kilograms, kg
$g$ is the gravitational field strength in newtons per kilogram, N/kg
$h$ is the change in height in metres, m.

> **1** *What is the increase in $E_p$ when a mass of 40 kg is lifted 8 m vertically?*

- **Power** is the rate of transfer of energy. Power can be calculated using the equation:

$$P = \frac{E}{t}$$

Where:
$P$ is the power in watts, W
$E$ is the energy in joules, J
$t$ is the time in seconds, s.

> **2** *It takes 2 seconds to lift the object in Question 1. What is the power developed?*

Student Book
pages 138–139 **P2**

# 3.3 Kinetic energy

## Key points

- The kinetic energy of a moving object depends on its mass and its speed.
- $E_k = \frac{1}{2} \times m \times v^2$
- Elastic potential energy is the energy stored in an elastic object when work is done on the object.

- All moving objects have **kinetic energy.** The greater the mass and the faster the speed of an object, the more kinetic energy it has.
- Kinetic energy can be calculated using the equation:

$$E_k = \frac{1}{2} \times m \times v^2$$

Where:
$E_k$ is the kinetic energy in joules, J
$m$ is the mass in kilograms, kg
$v$ is the speed in metres per second, m/s.

**▶ 1** *A boy of mass 40 kg runs at a speed of 5 m/s. What is his kinetic energy?*

- An object is described as being **elastic** if it regains its shape after being stretched or squashed. When work is done on an elastic object to stretch or squash it, the energy transferred to it is stored as **elastic potential energy**. When the object returns to its original shape, this energy is released.

**▶ 2** *When a spring is squashed and released it warms up. Why?*

**Key words:** kinetic energy, elastic potential energy

### Bump up your grade

If an elastic band is stretched and released, elastic potential energy is transferred to kinetic energy.

---

Student Book
pages 140–141 **P2**

# 3.4 Momentum

## Key points

- $p = m \times v$
- The unit of momentum is kg m/s.
- Momentum is conserved whenever objects interact, provided no external forces act on them.

- All moving objects have **momentum**. The greater the mass and the greater the velocity of an object, the greater its momentum.

**▶ 1** *When do objects have momentum?*

- Momentum can be calculated using the equation:

$$p = m \times v$$

Where:
$p$ is the momentum in kilogram metres per second, kg m/s
$m$ is the mass in kilograms, kg
$v$ is the velocity in metres per second, m/s.

### AQA Examiner's tip

Remember that momentum has a size and a direction.

**▶ 2** *What is the momentum of a 1000 kg car travelling at 30 m/s?*

- Whenever objects interact, the total momentum before the interaction is equal to the total momentum afterwards – provided no external forces act on them.
- This is called the law of **conservation of momentum.**
- Another way to say this is that the total change in momentum is zero.
- The interaction could be a collision or an explosion. After a collision the objects may move off together, or they may move apart.

**Key words:** momentum, conservation of momentum

### Bump up your grade

The unit of momentum is kg m/s, or you may see this written as Ns.

## 3.5 Explosions

Student Book
pages 142–143 **P2**

### Key points

- Momentum = mass × velocity; and velocity is speed in a certain direction.
- When two objects push each other apart, they move apart:
  - with different speeds if they have unequal masses
  - with equal and opposite momentum so their total momentum is zero.

**An artillery gun in action**

- Like velocity, momentum has both size and direction.
- In calculations, one direction must be defined as positive, so momentum in the opposite direction is negative.
- When two objects are at rest their momentum is zero. In an explosion the objects move apart with equal and opposite momentum. One momentum is positive and the other negative, so the total momentum after the explosion is zero.
- Firing a bullet from a gun is an example of an explosion. The bullet moves off with a momentum in one direction and the gun 'recoils' with equal momentum in the opposite direction.

**1** *What is the total momentum after an explosion equal to?*

**2** *Two students on roller skates stand holding each other in the playground. They push each other away. What can you say about the momentum of each student?*

**AQA** *Examiner's tip*

In calculations involving the conservation of momentum and collisions or explosions, it often helps if you sketch a diagram to show where the objects are before and after the collision or explosion.

## 3.6 Impact forces

Student Book
pages 144–145 **P2**

### Key points

- When vehicles collide, the force of the impact depends on mass, change of velocity and the duration of the impact.
- When two vehicles collide:
  - they exert equal and opposite forces on each other
  - their total momentum is unchanged.

*Bump up your grade*

Make sure that you can explain how crumple zones in cars reduce the forces acting by increasing the time taken to change the momentum of a car.

- When a force acts on an object that is able to move, or is moving, its momentum changes.
- For a particular change in momentum the longer the time taken for the change, the smaller the force that acts.
- In a collision, the momentum of an object often becomes zero during the impact – the object comes to rest.
- If the **impact time** is short, the forces on the object are large. As the impact time increases, the forces become less.

**1** *What is impact time?*

**Crumple zones** in cars are designed to fold in a collision. This increases the impact time and so reduces the force on the car and the people in it.

**2** *Why do cars have crumple zones at both the front and the rear?*

**Key words:** impact time, crumple zone

Student Book
pages 146–147
**P2**

# 3.7 Car safety

## Key points

- Seat belts and air bags spread the force across the chest and they also increase the impact time.

- Side impact bars and crumple zones 'give way' in an impact so increasing the impact time.

- We can use the conservation of momentum to find the speed of a car before an impact.

An airbag in action

- Modern cars contain a number of safety features designed to reduce the forces on the occupants of the car in a collision.

- Side impact bars and crumple zones fold up in a collision to increase the impact time and reduce the forces acting.

- **Seat belts** and **air bags** spread the forces on the body across a larger area. If a driver's head hits an airbag it changes momentum slowly, so the force on the head is less than it would be if it changed momentum quickly by hitting the steering wheel.

- A seat belt stops the wearer being flung forward if the car stops suddenly. The seatbelt stretches slightly increasing the impact time and reducing the force.

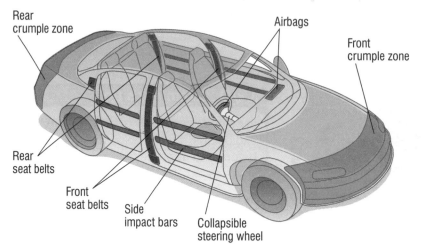

Rear crumple zone

Airbags

Front crumple zone

Rear seat belts

Front seat belts

Side impact bars

Collapsible steering wheel

**Car safety features**

> **1** *What happens to a passenger in a head-on collision:*
> **a** *if they are not wearing a seat belt?*
> **b** *if they were wearing a very narrow seat belt?*

After a car crash the police use measurements from the scene and the conservation of momentum to calculate the speed of the vehicles before the collision.

**AQA** *Examiner's tip*

Make sure that you can explain how different vehicle safety features work in terms of spreading out and reducing the forces on the occupants of the vehicle.

**1** When is work done by a force?

**2** What is the relationship between work and energy?

**3** What is the unit of power?

**4** What is the decrease in gravitational potential energy when an object of mass 6 kg is lowered through a distance of 9 m?

**5** What is elastic potential energy?

**6** What is the kinetic energy of a car of mass 1200 kg travelling at 30 m/s?

**7** What is the unit of momentum?

**8** What is the momentum of a 2500 kg truck travelling at 20 m/s?

**9** Why is a gymnast less likely to injure herself if she lands on a thick foam mat than if she lands on a hard floor?

**10** An electric motor is used to raise a 0.1 kg mass vertically upwards. If the mass gains 2 J of gravitational potential energy, calculate the height it is raised through.  [H]

**11** The electronic motor in Question 10 has a power of 1.5 W. Calculate the time taken to raise the load.  [H]

**12** A trolley of mass 0.2 kg travelling at 1.5 m/s to the right collides with a stationary trolley of mass 0.3 kg. After the collision they move off together. Calculate the velocity of the trolleys after the collision.  [H]

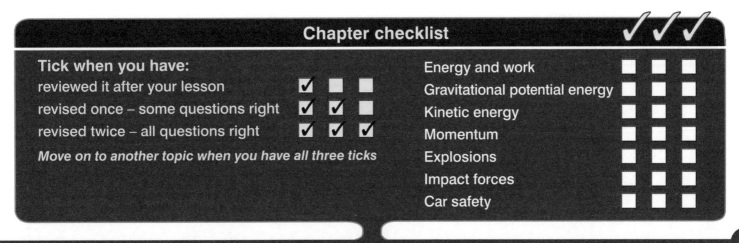

| Chapter checklist | | | ✓ ✓ ✓ |
|---|---|---|---|
| **Tick when you have:** | | | Energy and work  ☐ ☐ ☐ |
| reviewed it after your lesson | ☑ ☐ ☐ | | Gravitational potential energy  ☐ ☐ ☐ |
| revised once – some questions right | ☑ ☑ ☐ | | Kinetic energy  ☐ ☐ ☐ |
| revised twice – all questions right | ☑ ☑ ☑ | | Momentum  ☐ ☐ ☐ |
| *Move on to another topic when you have all three ticks* | | | Explosions  ☐ ☐ ☐ |
| | | | Impact forces  ☐ ☐ ☐ |
| | | | Car safety  ☐ ☐ ☐ |

Student Book
pages 150–151

**P2**

# 4.1 Electrical charges

## Key points

- Certain insulating materials become charged when rubbed together.
- Electrons are transferred when objects become charged.
- Like charges repel; unlike charges attract.

- When two electrically **insulating** materials are rubbed together, **electrons** are rubbed off one material and deposited on the other. Which way the electrons are transferred depends on the particular materials.
- Electrons have a **negative** charge so the material that has gained electrons becomes negatively charged. The one that has lost electrons is left with a **positive** charge. This process is called charging by friction.

▸ **1** *How does an insulator become negatively charged?*

- Two objects that have opposite electric charges **attract** each other. Two objects that have the same electric charges **repel** each other.
- The bigger the distance between the objects, the weaker the force between them.

▸ **2** *What will happen if two negatively charged objects are brought close together?*

**Key words:** insulating, electron, attract, repel

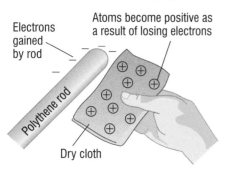

Electrons gained by rod

Atoms become positive as a result of losing electrons

Polythene rod

Dry cloth

**Charging by friction**

Student Book
pages 152–153

**P2**

# 4.2 Electric circuits

## Key points

- Every component has its own agreed symbol.
- $I = \dfrac{Q}{t}$

**AQA** *Examiner's tip*

Make sure that you can recognise and draw all of these circuit symbols. Use a sharp pencil and make sure there are no gaps or odd ends of wire shown on your diagram.

- Every component in a circuit has an agreed **circuit symbol**. These are put together in a circuit diagram to show how the components are connected together in a circuit.

$$I = \frac{Q}{t}$$

Where:
$I$ is the current in amperes, A
$Q$ is the charge in coulombs, C
$t$ is the time in seconds, s.

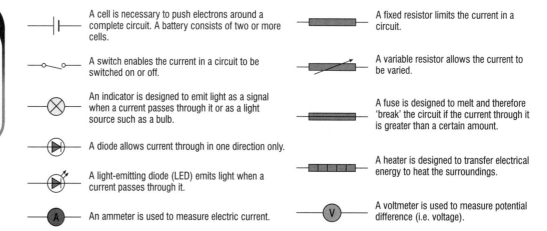

A cell is necessary to push electrons around a complete circuit. A battery consists of two or more cells.

A switch enables the current in a circuit to be switched on or off.

An indicator is designed to emit light as a signal when a current passes through it or as a light source such as a bulb.

A diode allows current through in one direction only.

A light-emitting diode (LED) emits light when a current passes through it.

An ammeter is used to measure electric current.

A fixed resistor limits the current in a circuit.

A variable resistor allows the current to be varied.

A fuse is designed to melt and therefore 'break' the circuit if the current through it is greater than a certain amount.

A heater is designed to transfer electrical energy to heat the surroundings.

A voltmeter is used to measure potential difference (i.e. voltage).

**Components and symbols**

▸ **1** *What is the circuit symbol for a closed switch?*
▸ **2** *What is the circuit symbol for a battery of three cells?*

Student Book
pages 154–155 **P2**

# 4.3 Resistance

## Key points

- $V = \dfrac{W}{Q} = \dfrac{E}{Q}$

- $R = \dfrac{V}{I}$

- Ohm's law states that the current through a resistor at constant temperature is directly proportional to the potential difference across the resistor.

- Reversing the current through a component reverses the potential difference across it.

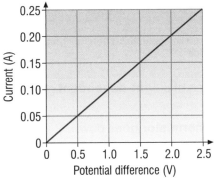

**A current–potential difference graph for a resistor**

AQA **Examiner's tip**

Ammeters are always connected in series and voltmeters are always connected in parallel.

- The current through a component is measured with an ammeter. Ammeters are always placed in **series** with the component. The unit of current is the ampere (or amp), A.

- The **potential difference** (pd), across a component is measured with a voltmeter. Voltmeters are always placed in **parallel** with the component. The unit of potential difference is the **volt, V**.

⟩⟩ **1** *What device is used to measure current?*

- Potential difference, work done and charge are related by the equation:

$$V = \frac{W}{Q}$$

Where:
$V$ is the potential difference in volts, V
$W$ is the work done in joules, J
$Q$ is the charge in coulombs, C.

- As work done is equal to energy transferred we can also say that:

$$V = \frac{E}{Q}$$

Where:
$E$ is the energy transferred in joules, J.

- **Resistance** is the opposition to current flow. The unit of resistance is the ohm, $\Omega$.

- The resistance of a component is calculated using the equation:

$$R = \frac{V}{I}$$

Where:
$R$ is resistance in ohms, $\Omega$
$V$ is potential difference in volts, V
$I$ is current in amps, A.

- Current–potential difference graphs are used to show how the current through a component varies with the potential difference across it.

## Ohm's law

- If a resistor is kept at a constant temperature, the current–potential difference graph shows a straight line passing through the origin. This means the current is directly proportional to the potential difference (pd) across the resistor. This is known as **Ohm's law**. Any component that obeys Ohm's law is called an **ohmic conductor**.

⟩⟩ **2** *What is the unit of resistance?*

**Key words:** series, potential difference, parallel, volt (V), resistance, Ohm's law, ohmic conductor

# 4.4 More current–potential difference graphs

- *Filament bulb:* resistance increases with increase of the filament temperature.
- *Diode:* 'forward' resistance low; 'reverse' resistance high.
- *Thermistor:* resistance decreases if its temperature increases.
- *LDR:* resistance decreases if the light intensity on it increases.

Current–potential difference may be plotted with the current on the *x*-axis or the *y*-axis. Make sure you know the shape either way round and check which way round they are given in exam questions.

- The line on a current–potential difference graph for a **filament bulb** is a curve. So the current is not directly proportional to the potential difference.
- The resistance of the filament increases as the current increases. This is because the resistance increases as the temperature increases.
- Reversing the potential difference makes no difference to the shape of the curve.
- The current through a **diode** flows in one direction only. In the reverse direction the diode has a very high resistance so the current is zero.

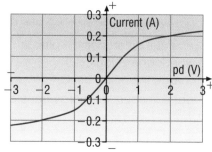

A current–potential difference graph for a filament bulb

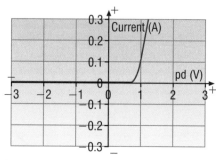

A current–potential difference graph for a diode

- As the light falling on it gets brighter, the resistance of a **light-dependent resistor** (LDR) decreases.
- As the temperature goes up, the resistance of a **thermistor** goes down.

> **1** What happens to the resistance of an LDR if its surroundings become darker?
>
> **2** What effect does reversing the pd across a filament bulb have on the current–potential difference curve?

**Key words:** filament bulb, diode, light-dependent resistor, thermistor

# 4.5 Series circuits

- For components in series:
  - the current is the same in each component
  - adding the potential differences gives the total potential difference
  - adding the resistances gives the total resistance.

- In a **series** circuit the components are connected one after another. Therefore if there is a break anywhere in the circuit, charge stops flowing.
- There is no choice of route for the charge as it flows around the circuit, so the current through each component is the same.

> **1** What happens in a series circuit if one component stops working?

- The current depends on the potential difference (pd) of the **supply** and the total resistance of the circuit:

$$I = \frac{V}{R}$$

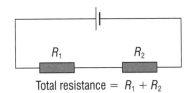

Total resistance $= R_1 + R_2$

**Resistors in series**

- The pd of the supply is shared between all the components in the circuit. So the pds across individual components add up to give the pd of the supply.
- The resistances of the individual components in series add up to give the total resistance of the circuit.
- The bigger the resistance of a component, the bigger its share of the supply pd.

▶ **2** *How could you find the total resistance in a series circuit?*

---

Student Book
pages 160–161 **P2**

# 4.6 Parallel circuits

## Key points

- For components in parallel:
  - the total current is the sum of the currents through the separate components
  - the bigger the resistance of a component the smaller the current is.

- In a parallel circuit the potential difference is the same across each component.

- To calculate the current through a resistor in a parallel circuit use $I = \dfrac{V}{R}$

- In a **parallel** circuit each component is connected across the supply, so if there is a break in one part of the circuit, charge can still flow in the other parts.
- Each component is connected across the supply pd, so the pd across each component is the same.
- There are junctions in the circuit so different amounts of charge can flow through different components. The current through each component depends on its resistance. The bigger the resistance of a component, the smaller the current through it.

▶ **1** *What happens in a parallel circuit if one component stops working?*

- The current through a component in a parallel circuit can be calculated using
$$I = \frac{V}{R}$$
- The total current through the whole circuit is equal to the sum of the currents through the separate components.

▶ **2** *In a parallel circuit what is the relationship between the supply pd and the pd across each parallel component?*

### Bump up your grade

In everyday life, parallel circuits are much more useful than series circuits. That is because a break in one part of the circuit does not stop charge flowing in the rest of the circuit.

### Maths skills

Two $4\,\Omega$ resistors are connected in parallel across a 12 V battery. Calculate the total current through the battery.

pd across each resistor = pd across the battery

For each resistor $V = I \times R$
$$I = \frac{V}{R}$$
$$I = \frac{12\,V}{4\,\Omega}$$
$$I = 3\,A$$

Total current $= 3\,A + 3\,A = 6\,A$

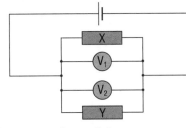

**Components in parallel**

### AQA Examiner's tip

Make sure that you understand the difference between series and parallel circuits.

**1** What sort of charge does an electron have?

**2** In terms of electrons, how does an insulator become positively charged?

**3** What sort of force will there be between two negatively charged objects?

**4** Draw a circuit diagram for a circuit containing a cell, a bulb, a resistor and a switch, connected one after the other.

**5** If the current through a component is 0.2 A when the potential difference across it is 12 V, what is its resistance?

**6** The energy transferred to a bulb is 36 J when 8.0 C of charge passes through it. Calculate the potential difference across the bulb.

**7** What is an ohmic conductor?

**8** Explain the shape of the line on a current–potential difference graph for a diode.

**9** A series circuit contains a variable resistor. If its resistance is increased, what happens to the pd across it?

**10** A 5 Ω resistor and an 8 Ω resistor are connected in series. What is their total resistance?

**11** Where should an ammeter and a voltmeter be placed in a circuit to measure the current through, and the pd across, a resistor?

**12** A 4 Ω resistor and a 12 Ω resistor are connected in series with a 12 V battery. What is the current in the circuit?

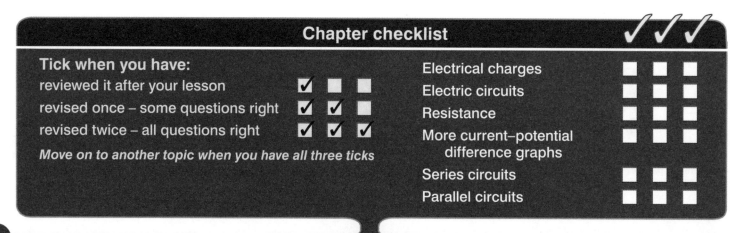

**Chapter checklist**  ✓ ✓ ✓

**Tick when you have:**
reviewed it after your lesson  ☑ ☐ ☐
revised once – some questions right  ☑ ☑ ☐
revised twice – all questions right  ☑ ☑ ☑
*Move on to another topic when you have all three ticks*

Electrical charges  ☐ ☐ ☐
Electric circuits  ☐ ☐ ☐
Resistance  ☐ ☐ ☐
More current–potential difference graphs  ☐ ☐ ☐
Series circuits  ☐ ☐ ☐
Parallel circuits  ☐ ☐ ☐

Student Book
pages 164–165

**P2**

# 5.1 Alternating current

- Cells and batteries supply current that passes round the circuit in one direction.
- This is called **direct current**, or dc.
- The current from the mains supply passes in one direction, then reverses and passes in the other direction.
- This is called **alternating current**, or ac.

**⟫ 1  What is direct current?**

- The **frequency** of the UK mains supply is 50 hertz (Hz), which means it changes direction 50 times each second. The 'voltage' of the mains is 230 V.
- The **live wire** of the mains supply alternates between a positive and a negative potential with respect to the **neutral wire**. The neutral wire stays at zero volts.
- The live wire alternates between **peak voltages** of +325 V and −325 V. In terms of electrical power, this is equivalent to a direct potential difference of 230 V.

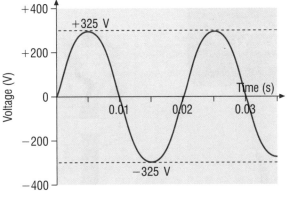

**Graph of mains voltage against time**

**⟫ 2  What is the potential of the neutral terminal?**

The frequency of an ac supply can be determined from an **oscilloscope** trace using the equation

$$f = \frac{1}{T}$$

Where:
$f$ is the frequency of the ac in hertz, Hz
$T$ is the time for one cycle in seconds, s

**Key words:** direct current, alternating current, frequency, live wire, neutral wire, oscilloscope

## Key points

- Direct current is in one direction only. Alternating current repeatedly reverses its direction.
- The peak voltage of an alternating potential difference is the maximum voltage measured from zero volts.
- A mains circuit has a live wire that is alternately positive and negative every cycle and a neutral wire at zero volts.

$$f = \frac{1}{T}$$  [H]

**Bump up your grade**

Make sure that you can make readings from diagrams of oscilloscope traces.

**Higher**

# 5.2 Cables and plugs

## Key points

- Sockets and plugs are made of stiff plastic materials, which enclose the electrical connections.

- Cables consist of two or three insulated copper wires surrounded by an outer layer of flexible plastic material.

- In a three-pin plug or a three-core cable:
  - the live wire is brown
  - the neutral wire is blue
  - the earth wire is green and yellow.

- The earth wire is used to earth the metal case of a mains appliance.

**Mains cable**

- Most electrical appliances are connected to the **sockets** of the mains supply using **cable** and a **three-pin plug**.

- The outer cover of a three-pin plug is made of plastic or rubber. Both these materials are good electrical insulators.

- The pins of the plug are made of brass. Brass is a good electrical conductor. It is also hard and will not rust or oxidise.

- The earth wire is connected to the longest pin.

- It is important that the cable grip is fastened tightly over the cable. There should be no bare wires showing inside the plug and the correct cable must be connected firmly to the terminal of the correct pin.

- The brown wire is connected to the live pin.

- The blue wire is connected to the neutral pin.

- The green and yellow wire (of a three-core cable) is connected to the earth pin. A two-core cable does not have an earth wire.

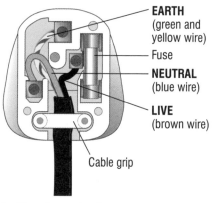

EARTH
(green and yellow wire)

Fuse

NEUTRAL
(blue wire)

LIVE
(brown wire)

Cable grip

**Inside a three-pin plug**

▐▐▐▶ **1**  *Why are the pins of a plug made of brass?*

- Appliances with metal cases must be earthed – the case is attached to the earth wire in the cable.

- Appliances with plastic cases do not need to be earthed. They are said to be double insulated and are connected to the supply with two-core cable containing just a live and a neutral wire.

▐▐▐▶ **2**  *Why must appliances with metal cases be earthed?*

- Cables of different thicknesses are used for different purposes. The more current to be carried, the thicker the cable needs to be.

**AQA** *Examiner's tip*

Make sure that you can identify faults in the wiring of a three-pin plug.

**Key words:** socket, cable, three-pin plug

Student Book
pages 168–169 **P2**

# 5.3 Fuses

Student Book
pages 168–169

### Key points

- A fuse contains a thin wire that heats up and melts if too much current passes through it. This cuts off the current.
- A circuit breaker is an electromagnetic switch that opens (i.e. 'trips' ) and cuts the current off if too much current passes through it.

### Bump up your grade

Make sure you can explain how the earth wire and the fuse wire work together to protect an appliance.

- A mains appliance with a plastic case does not need to be earthed because plastic is an insulator and cannot become live.
- Appliances with metal cases need to be earthed. Otherwise if a fault develops, and the live wire touches the metal case, the case becomes live and could give a shock to anyone who touches it.
- A **fuse** is always fitted in series with the live wire. This cuts the appliance off from the live wire if the fuse blows.
- If a fault develops in an earthed appliance, a large current flows to earth and melts the fuse, disconnecting the supply.
- The rating of the fuse should be slightly higher than the normal working current of the appliance. If it is much higher, it will not melt soon enough. If it is not higher than the normal current, it will melt as soon as the appliance is switched on.

> **1** *What is a fuse?*

- A **circuit breaker** can be used in place of a fuse. This is an electromagnetic switch that opens and cuts off the supply if the current is bigger than a certain value.

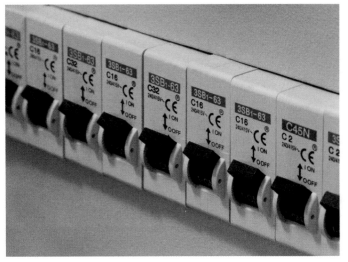

**A circuit breaker**

- A **residual current circuit breaker (RCCB)** cuts off the current in the live wire if it is different to the current in the neutral wire. It works faster than a fuse or an ordinary circuit breaker.

> **2** *Why don't appliances with plastic cases need to be earthed?*

**Key words:** fuse, circuit breaker, residual current circuit breaker (RCCB)

# 5.4 Electrical power and potential difference

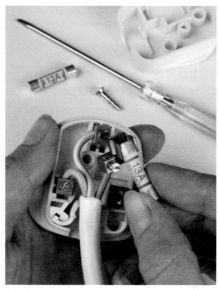

**Changing a fuse**

- An electrical appliance transfers electrical energy into other forms of energy.
- The rate at which it does this is called the power.
- Power can be calculated using the equation:

$$P = \frac{E}{t}$$

Where:
$P$ is the power in watts, W
$E$ is the energy transferred in joules, J
$t$ is the time in seconds, s.

**1** *What is the power, in kW, of an appliance that transfers 90 000 J of energy in 30 seconds?*

In an electric circuit it is more usual to measure the current through an appliance and the potential difference across it rather than the energy transferred and the time.

We can also use current and pd to calculate the power of the appliance using the equation:

$$P = I \times V$$

Where:
$P$ is the power in watts, W
$I$ is the current in amperes, A
$V$ is the potential difference in volts, V.

- Electrical appliances have their power rating shown on them. The pd of the mains supply is 230 V.
- This equation can be used to calculate the normal current through an appliance and so work out the size of fuse to use.
- The fuse is chosen so that its value is slightly higher than the calculated current.

**Maths skills**

What is the current in a steam wallpaper stripper that has a power of 2 kW?

$P = I \times V$

$I = \dfrac{P}{V}$

$I = 2000\,\text{W}/230\,\text{V}$

$I = 8.7\,\text{A}$

**2** *What is the power of a mains appliance that takes a current of 10 A?*

Student Book
pages 172–173 **P2**

# 5.5 Electrical energy and charge

- An electric current is the rate of flow of **charge**.
- The equation relating charge, current and time is:

$$Q = I \times t$$

Where:
$Q$ is the charge in coulombs, C
$I$ is the current in amperes, A
$t$ is the time in seconds, s.

> ▶ **1** *How much charge flows past a particular point in a circuit when a current of 2A flows for 2 minutes?*

- When charge flows through an appliance, electrical energy is transferred to other forms. In a resistor, electrical energy is transferred to the resistor so the resistor becomes hotter.

## Energy, potential difference and charge

The amount of energy transferred can be calculated using the equation:

$$E = V \times Q$$

Where:
$E$ is the energy in joules, J
$V$ is the potential difference in volts, V
$Q$ is the charge in coulombs, C.

> ▶ **2** *How much energy is transferred when a charge of 200 C flows through a resistor that has a potential difference across it of 230V?*

*Higher*

### Key points

- An electric current is the rate of flow of charge.
- $Q = I \times t$
- When charge flows through a resistor, energy transferred to the resistor makes it hot.
- $E = V \times Q$ **[H]**

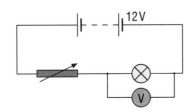

Energy transfer in a circuit

### AQA Examiner's tip

When a charge flows in a circuit the components will heat up. This means that most electrical appliances have vents to keep them cool.

---

Student Book
pages 174–175 **P2**

# 5.6 Electrical issues ⚙

- **Electrical faults** may occur as a result of damage to sockets, plugs, cables or appliances.
- Electrical equipment should be checked regularly for wear. Worn or damaged items should be replaced or repaired by a qualified electrician.
- Avoid overloading sockets, as this may cause overheating and a risk of fire.
- Electrical appliances should be handled safely and never used in a bathroom or with wet hands.
- The cable should always be appropriate for the intended use.

> ▶ **1** *Why can two-core cable be used for a hairdryer?*

- When choosing an electrical appliance, the power and efficiency rating need to be considered, as well as the cost.
- Filament bulbs and halogen bulbs are much less efficient than low-energy bulbs and do not last as long.
- There are a number of different low-energy bulbs available.

> ▶ **2** *Why are filament bulbs very inefficient?*

### Key points

- Electrical faults are dangerous because they can cause electric shocks and fires.
- Never touch a mains appliance (or plug or socket) with wet hands. Never touch a bare wire or a terminal at a potential of more than 30V.
- Check cables, plugs and sockets for damage regularly.

### AQA Examiner's tip

You may have to identify the best appliance to use in a particular situation from information given in a question.

**1** What is the potential difference of the mains supply?

**2** What is the frequency of the mains supply?

**3** What is the peak voltage of the mains supply?

**4** What colour is the neutral wire?

**5** What does the cover on an earth wire look like?

**6** Why is the outer cover of a three-pin plug made of plastic?

**7** What fuse should be used in a 500 W mains heater?

**8** What is the unit of charge?

**9** What is a circuit breaker?

**10** How much energy is transferred when a 2 kW appliance is used for 15 seconds?

**11** What is the current through a 2300 W mains heater?

**12** 24 000 J of energy are transferred when 2000 C of charge flow through a bulb. What is the potential difference across the bulb? [H]

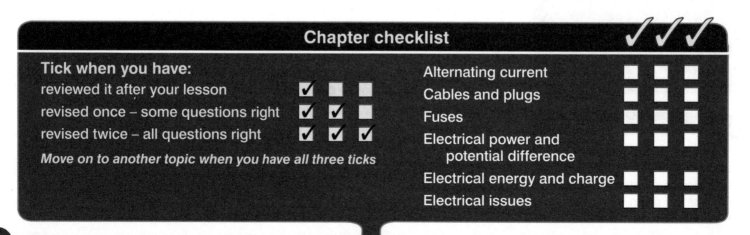

| Chapter checklist | ✔ | ✔ | ✔ |
|---|---|---|---|
| **Tick when you have:** | | | |
| reviewed it after your lesson | ✔ | ☐ | ☐ |
| revised once – some questions right | ✔ | ✔ | ☐ |
| revised twice – all questions right | ✔ | ✔ | ✔ |
| *Move on to another topic when you have all three ticks* | | | |
| Alternating current | ☐ | ☐ | ☐ |
| Cables and plugs | ☐ | ☐ | ☐ |
| Fuses | ☐ | ☐ | ☐ |
| Electrical power and potential difference | ☐ | ☐ | ☐ |
| Electrical energy and charge | ☐ | ☐ | ☐ |
| Electrical issues | ☐ | ☐ | ☐ |

Student Book
pages 178–179

**P2**

# 6.1 Observing nuclear radiation

- The basic structure of an atom is a small central **nucleus**, made up of **protons** and **neutrons**, surrounded by **electrons**.
- The nuclei of radioactive substances are unstable. They become stable by **radioactive decay**. In this process, they emit radiation and turn into other elements.
- The three types of radiation emitted are: **alpha radiation**, **beta radiation**, **gamma radiation**.

> **1** *Which part of an atom might emit alpha particles?*

- We cannot predict when an unstable nucleus will decay. It is a random process and is not affected by external conditions.
- **Background radiation** is around us all the time. This is radiation from radioactive substances in the environment, from space, from devices such as X-ray tubes.

> **2** *What happens to the rate of radioactive decay if the temperature is doubled?*

**Key words:** nucleus, proton, neutron, electron, alpha radiation, beta radiation, gamma radiation

---

Student Book
pages 180–181

**P2**

# 6.2 The discovery of the nucleus

- At one time scientists thought that atoms consisted of spheres of positive charge with electrons stuck into them, like plums in a pudding. So this became known as the 'plum pudding' model of the atom.
- Then Rutherford, Geiger and Marsden devised an **alpha particle scattering** experiment, in which they fired alpha particles at thin gold foil.
- Most of the alpha particles passed straight through the foil. This means that most of the atom is just empty space.
- Some of the alpha particles were deflected through small angles. This suggests that the nucleus has a positive charge.
- A few rebound through very large angles. This suggests that the nucleus has a large mass and a very large positive charge.

> **1** *Why did most alpha particles pass straight through the foil in Rutherford's experiment?*
> **2** *What did the alpha particle scattering experiment suggest about the structure of the nucleus?*

### Bump up your grade

The alpha particle has a positive charge. Because some of the alpha particles rebound, they must be repelled by another positive charge.

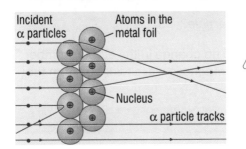

Incident α particles — Atoms in the metal foil — Nucleus — α particle tracks

**Alpha particle scattering**

# 6.3 Nuclear reactions

## Key points

- Isotopes of an element are atoms with the same number of protons but different numbers of neutrons. Therefore they have the same atomic numbers but different mass numbers.

**AQA** *Examiner's tip*

Make sure you can use nuclear equations to show how the atomic number and mass number change when alpha or beta particles are emitted. **[H]**

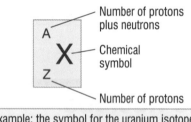

Example: the symbol for the uranium isotope with 92 protons and 146 neutrons is

$$^{238}_{\ 92}U \text{ (or sometimes U-238)}$$

**Representing an isotope**

|  | Change in the nucleus | Particle emitted |
|---|---|---|
| α decay | The nucleus loses 2 protons and 2 neutrons | 2 protons and 2 neutrons emitted as an α particle |
| β decay | A neutron in the nucleus changes into a proton and an electron | The electron created in the nucleus is instantly emitted |

- The table below gives the relative masses and charges of these particles.

|  | Relative mass | Relative charge |
|---|---|---|
| Proton | 1 | +1 |
| Neutron | 1 | 0 |
| Electron | 0.0005 | −1 |

- In an atom the number of protons = number of electrons, so the atom has no overall charge. If an atom loses or gains electrons it becomes charged and is called an **ion**.
- All atoms of a particular element have the same number of protons. Atoms of the same element with different numbers of neutrons are called **isotopes**.
- The number of protons in an atom is its **atomic number**.
- The total number of protons plus neutrons in an atom is its **mass number**.
- An alpha particle consists of two protons and two neutrons. It has a relative mass of 4 and its relative charge is +2. We represent it as $^4_2\alpha$.

When a nucleus emits an alpha particle the atomic number goes down by two and the mass number goes down by four.

For example, radium emits an alpha particle and becomes radon.

**1** *What is the relative charge of an alpha particle?*

- A beta particle is a high-speed electron from the nucleus, emitted when a neutron in the nucleus changes to a proton and an electron. Its relative mass is 0 and its relative charge is −1. We represent it as $^{\ 0}_{-1}\beta$.

The proton stays in the nucleus so the atomic number goes up by one and the mass number is unchanged. The electron is instantly emitted.

For example, carbon-14 emits a beta particle when it becomes nitrogen.

**2** *What is the relative charge of a beta particle?*

- When a nucleus emits gamma radiation there is no change in the atomic number or the mass number. A gamma ray is an electromagnetic wave released from the nucleus. It has no charge and no mass.

**Key words:** ion, isotope, atomic number, mass number

Student Book
pages 184–185 **P2**

# 6.4 More about alpha, beta and gamma radiation

- When nuclear radiation travels through a material it will collide with the atoms of the material.

- This knocks electrons off them, creating ions. This is called **ionisation**.

- Ionisation in a living cell can damage or kill the cell.

- **Alpha particles** are relatively large, so they have lots of collisions with atoms – they are strongly ionising.

- Because of these collisions, the alpha particles do not penetrate far into a material.

- They can be stopped by a thin sheet of paper, human skin or a few centimetres of air.

- Alpha particles have a positive charge and are deflected by **electric and magnetic fields**.

- **Beta particles** are much smaller and faster than alpha particles so they are less ionising and penetrate further.

- They are blocked by a few metres of air or a thin sheet of aluminium.

- Beta particles have a negative charge and are deflected by electric and magnetic fields in the opposite direction to alpha particles.

- **Gamma rays** are electromagnetic waves so they will travel a long way through a material before colliding with an atom.

- They are weakly ionising and very penetrating.

- Several centimetres of lead or several metres of concrete are needed to absorb most of the radiation.

- Gamma rays are not deflected by electric and magnetic fields.

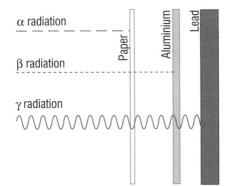

**The penetrating powers of α, β and γ radiation**

 **1** *Which type of nuclear radiation is the least penetrating?*
**2** *Which type of nuclear radiation is the least ionising?*

**Key word:** ionisation

# 6.5 Half-life

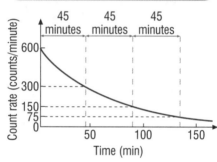

Radioactive decay: a graph of count rate against time

- We can measure the radioactivity of a sample of a radioactive material by measuring the **count rate** from it.
- The radioactivity of a sample decreases over time. How quickly the count rate falls to nearly zero depends on the isotope. Some take a few minutes, others take millions of years.

▶ **1** *What happens to the count rate of a radioactive sample over time?*

- We use the idea of **half-life** to measure how quickly the radioactivity decreases. It is the time taken for the count rate from the original isotope to fall to half its initial value.
- Or we can define it as the time it takes for the number of unstable nuclei in a sample to halve.
- The half-life is the same for any sample of a particular isotope.

▶ **2** *What has happened to the original count rate of a radioactive sample after two half-lives have passed?*

**Key word:** half-life

---

# 6.6 Radioactivity at work

- **Alpha sources** are used in smoke alarms. The alpha particles are not dangerous because they are very poorly penetrating. The source needs a half-life of several years.
- **Beta sources** are used for **thickness monitoring** in the manufacture of things like paper or metal foil. Alpha particles would be stopped by a thin sheet of paper and all gamma rays would pass through it. The source needs a half-life of many years, so that decreases in count rate are due to changes in the thickness of the paper.
- **Gamma and beta sources** are used as **tracers** in medicine. The source is injected or swallowed by the patient. Its progress around the body is monitored by a detector outside the patient. The source needs a half-life of a few hours so that the patient is not exposed to unnecessary radioactivity.

▶ **1** *Why isn't an alpha source used as a tracer in medicine?*

- **Radioactive dating** is used to find the age of ancient material. Carbon dating is used to find the age of wood and other organic material. Uranium dating is used to find the age of igneous rocks.

▶ **2** *Why do medical tracers have half-lives of just a few hours?*

**Key words:** tracer, radioactive dating

1  What is the effect of pressure on the rate of radioactive decay?

2  What is background radiation?

3  What was Rutherford's alpha particle scattering experiment?

4  What happens to the mass number of a nucleus when it emits a beta particle?

5  What happens to the atomic number of a nucleus when it emits a beta particle?

6  What happens to the mass number of a nucleus when it emits an alpha particle?

7  What happens to the atomic number of a nucleus when it emits an alpha particle?

8  Why is gamma radiation **not** deflected by electric and magnetic fields?

9  What has happened to the number of atoms undergoing nuclear decay in a sample after three half-lives have passed?

10  Why is alpha radiation unsuitable for monitoring the thickness of metal foil?

11  A radioactive isotope has a half-life of seven hours. A sample of the isotope has a mass of 4 milligrams. What mass of the isotope has decayed after 14 hours?

12  A sample of a radioactive isotope contains 100 000 atoms of the isotope. How many atoms of the isotope will remain after three half-lives?

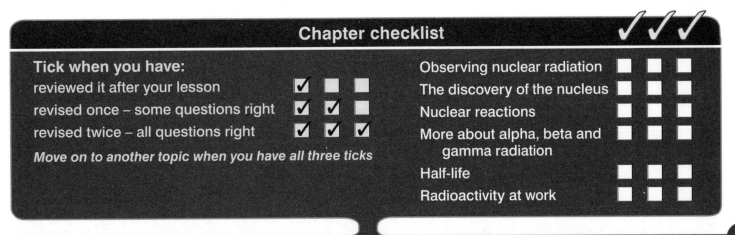

Chapter checklist

Tick when you have:
reviewed it after your lesson  ☑ ☐ ☐
revised once – some questions right  ☑ ☑ ☐
revised twice – all questions right  ☑ ☑ ☑
*Move on to another topic when you have all three ticks*

Observing nuclear radiation  ☐ ☐ ☐
The discovery of the nucleus  ☐ ☐ ☐
Nuclear reactions  ☐ ☐ ☐
More about alpha, beta and gamma radiation  ☐ ☐ ☐
Half-life  ☐ ☐ ☐
Radioactivity at work  ☐ ☐ ☐

Student Book
pages 192–193

**P2**

# 7.1 Nuclear fission

## Key points

- Nuclear fission is the splitting of a nucleus into two approximately equal fragments and the release of two or three neutrons.

- Nuclear fission occurs when a neutron hits a uranium-235 nucleus or a plutonium-239 nucleus and the nucleus splits.

- A chain reaction occurs when neutrons from the fission go on to cause other fission events.

- In a nuclear reactor control rods absorb fission neutrons to ensure that, on average, only one neutron per fission goes on to produce further fission.

- **Nuclear fission** is the splitting of an atomic nucleus.
- There are two fissionable isotopes in common use in nuclear reactors, uranium-235 and plutonium-239. The majority of nuclear reactors use uranium-235.
- Naturally occurring uranium is mostly uranium-238, which is non-fissionable. Most nuclear reactors use 'enriched' uranium that contains 2–3% uranium-235.
- For fission to occur, the uranium-235 or plutonium-239 nucleus must absorb a neutron. The nucleus then splits into two smaller nuclei. In this process two or three neutrons are emitted and energy is released. The energy released in such a nuclear process is much greater than the energy released in a chemical process such as burning.
- A **chain reaction** occurs when each fission event causes further fission events. In a nuclear reactor the process is controlled, so one fission neutron per fission on average goes on to produce further fission.

> **1** What is enriched uranium?
> **2** What happens for fission to occur?

**AQA** *Examiner's tip*

Make sure that you can draw a simple diagram to show a chain reaction.

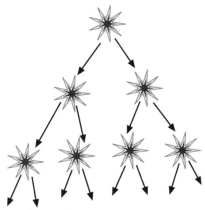

In a chain reaction, each reaction causes more reactions which cause more reactions, etc. etc.

**A chain reaction**

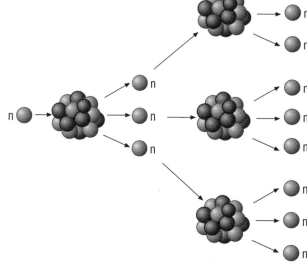

**A chain reaction in a nuclear reactor**

**Key words:** nuclear fission, chain reaction

Student Book
pages 194–195 **P2**

# 7.2 Nuclear fusion

- **Nuclear fusion** is the process of forcing two nuclei close enough together so they form a single larger nucleus.
- Nuclear fusion can be brought about by making two light nuclei collide at very high speed. Fusion is the process by which energy is released in stars.
- There are enormous problems with producing energy from nuclear fusion in reactors. Nuclei approaching each other will repel one another due to their positive charge. To overcome this, the nuclei must be heated to very high temperatures to give them enough energy to overcome the repulsion and fuse. Because of the enormously high temperatures involved, the reaction cannot take place in a normal 'container', but has to be contained by a magnetic field.

## Key points

- Nuclear fusion is the process of forcing two nuclei close enough together so they form a single larger nucleus.
- Energy is released when two light nuclei are fused together.

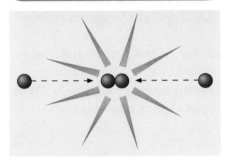

**A nuclear fusion reaction**

▐▐▶ **1** *By what process is energy released in stars?*

▐▐▶ **2** *How are nuclei contained in a fusion reactor?*

**AQA** *Examiner's tip*

In an examination, students often confuse fission and fusion. Make sure that you can explain the difference between them.

**Key word:** nuclear fusion

Student Book
pages 196–197 **P2**

# 7.3 Nuclear issues ⚙️

- The major source of background **radiation** is radon gas which seeps through the ground from radioactive substances in rocks deep underground. Radon gas emits alpha particles, so is a health hazard if breathed in.
- Other sources of background radiation include cosmic rays from outer space, food and drink, air travel, and nuclear weapons testing.
- Medical sources of background radiation include X-rays, as these have an ionising effect, as well as radioactive substances.

## Key points

- Radon gas is an $\alpha$-emitting isotope that seeps into houses in certain areas through the ground.
- There are thousands of fission reactors safely in use throughout the world. None of them are of the same type as the Chernobyl reactors that exploded.
- Nuclear waste is stored in safe and secure conditions for many years after unused uranium and plutonium (to be used in the future) is removed from it.

▐▐▶ **1** *What is the major source of background radiation?*

- Uranium and plutonium are chemically removed from used fuel rods from nuclear reactors, as these substances can be used again. The remaining radioactive waste must be stored in secure conditions for many years.
- To reduce exposure to nuclear radiations, workers should:
  - keep as far as possible from sources of radiation–
  - spend as little time exposed as possible
  - shield themselves with materials such as concrete and lead.

▐▐▶ **2** *Why must radioactive waste be stored securely?*

# 7.4  The early universe

## Key points

- A galaxy is a collection of billions of stars held together by their own gravity.

- Before galaxies and stars formed, the universe was formed of hydrogen and helium.

- The force of gravity pulled matter into galaxies and stars.

- Most scientists believe that the universe was created by the Big Bang about 13 thousand million (13 billion) years ago. At first the universe was a hot glowing ball of radiation. In the first few minutes the nuclei of the lightest elements formed. As the universe expanded, over millions of years, its temperature fell. Uncharged atoms were formed.

**1** *What happened to the temperature of the universe as it expanded?*

- Before galaxies and stars formed, the universe was a dark patchy cloud of hydrogen and helium. Eventually dust and gas were pulled together by **gravitational attraction** to form **stars**. The resulting intense heat started off nuclear fusion reactions in the stars, so they began to emit visible light and other radiation.

- Very large groups of stars are called galaxies. Our Sun is one of the many billions of stars in the Milky Way galaxy. The universe contains billions of galaxies.

- A galaxy is a collection of billions of stars held together by their own gravity. There are billions of galaxies in the universe, with vast empty space between them.

**2** *What is a galaxy?*

### Bump up your grade

You should understand that the distance between neighbouring stars is usually millions of times greater than the distance between planets in our Solar System. The distance between neighbouring galaxies is usually millions of times greater than the distance between stars within a galaxy. So the universe is mostly empty space.

**Andromeda – the nearest big galaxy to the Milky Way**

**Key words:** gravitational attraction, star

# 7.5 The life history of a star

**AQA** *Examiner's tip*

Exam questions may ask you to put the stages of the life cycle of a star in the correct order, so make sure you learn them thoroughly.

- Gravitational forces pull clouds of dust and gas together to form a **protostar**.
- The protostar becomes denser and the nuclei of hydrogen atoms and other light elements start to **fuse** together. Energy is released in the process so the core gets hotter and brighter.
- Stars radiate energy because of hydrogen fusion in the core. This stage can continue for billions of years until the star runs out of hydrogen nuclei. The star is stable because the inward force of gravity is balanced by the outward force of radiation from the core and is called a **main sequence star**.
- Eventually a star runs out of hydrogen nuclei, swells, cools down and turns red.

**⟫ 1** *Why are stars in the main sequence stable?*

- What happens next in the life cycle of the star depends on its size.
- A star similar in size to our Sun (low mass) is now a **red giant**.
- Helium and other light elements fuse to form heavier elements.
- Fusion stops and the star will contract to form a **white dwarf**.
- Eventually no more light is emitted and the star becomes a **black dwarf**.
- A star much larger than the Sun will swell to become a red **supergiant** which continues to collapse.
- Eventually the star explodes in a **supernova**. The outer layers are thrown out into space. The core is left as a **neutron star**.
- If this is massive enough it becomes a **black hole**. The gravitational field of a black hole is so strong not even light can escape from it.

**⟫ 2** *What is a neutron star?*

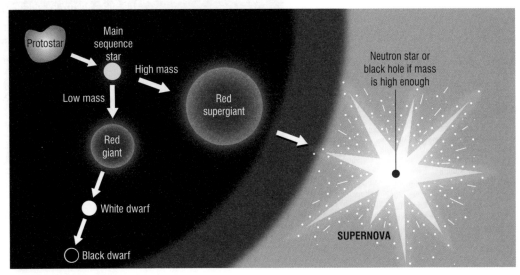

The life cycle of a star

**Key words:** protostar, main sequence star, red giant, white dwarf, black dwarf, supergiant, supernova, neutron star, black hole

# 7.6 How the chemical elements formed

## Key points

- Elements as heavy as iron are formed inside stars as a result of nuclear fusion.

- Elements heavier than iron are formed in supernovas, along with lighter elements.

- The Sun and the rest of the Solar System were formed from the debris of a supernova.

### Bump up your grade

In the process of fusion, light nuclei fuse to form heavier nuclei and energy is released. For elements heavier than iron to be formed there must be an input of energy.

- Chemical elements are formed by fusion processes in stars. The nuclei of lighter elements fuse to form the nuclei of heavier elements. The process releases large amounts of energy.

- Elements heavier than iron are only formed in the final stages of the life of a big star. This is because the process requires the input of energy. All the elements get distributed through space by the supernova explosion.

- The presence of the heavier elements in the Sun and inner planets is evidence that they were formed from debris scattered by a supernova.

1 **What is the heaviest element formed by fusion in a main sequence star?**

2 **How are the chemical elements distributed through space?**

Gas, rocks and dust

The Sun forms at the centre of a spinning cloud of dust, gas and rock.

Gas

Rocks

The Sun's energy evaporates ice and drives gas away from the inner Solar System, leaving rocks behind.

The rocky planets form near the Sun and the gas giant planets form further away. The minor planet Pluto orbits the Sun beyond the giant planets.

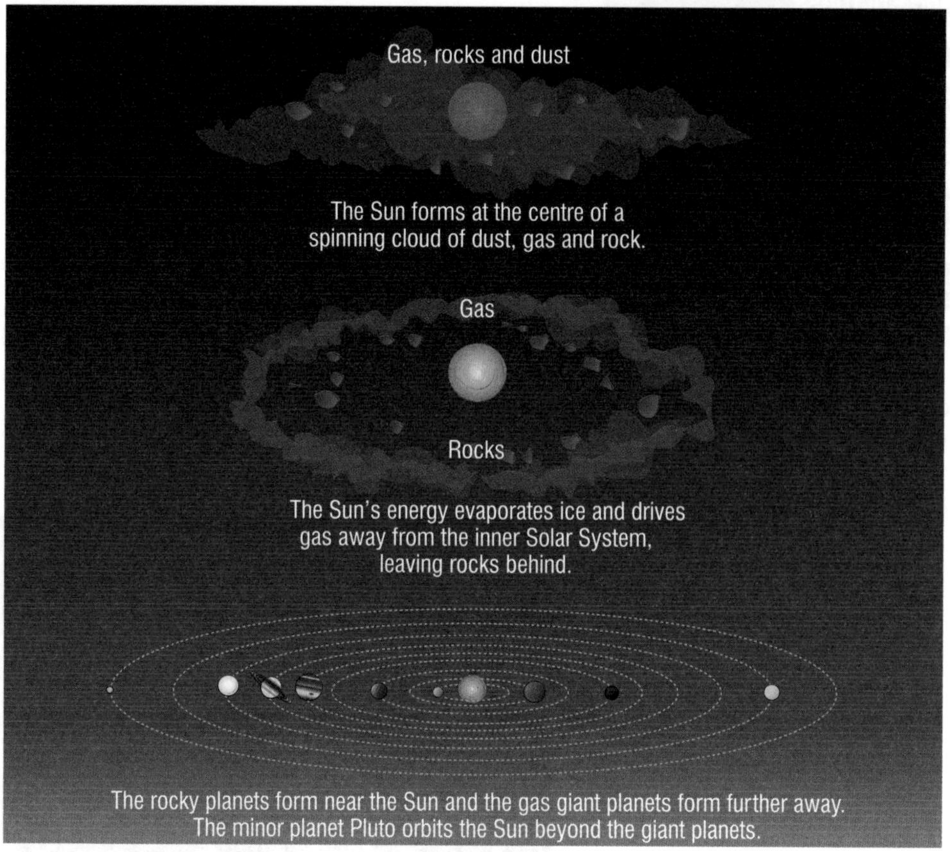

**Formation of the Solar System**

**1** What is a fissionable isotope?

**2** Which two fissionable isotopes are used in nuclear reactors?

**3** When does a chain reaction occur?

**4** What is nuclear fusion?

**5** How can nuclei be made to come close enough to fuse?

**6** How long did it take for the temperature of the universe to fall enough so that uncharged atoms were formed?

**7** Why is a black hole black?

**8** When is a black hole formed?

**9** What will the final stage in the life cycle of the Sun be?

**10** What evidence is there that the Sun and inner planets formed from the remnants of a supernova?

**11** What is the name of the process that produces the chemical elements?

**12** When are elements heavier than iron formed?

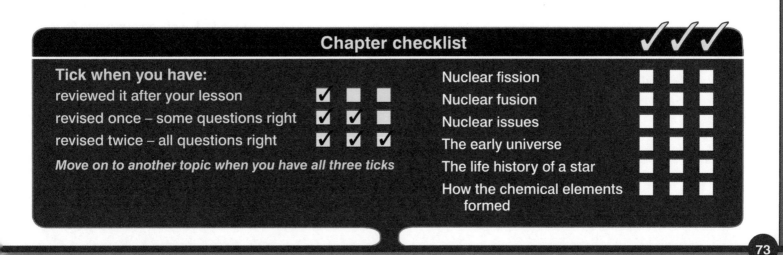

**Chapter checklist** ✓ ✓ ✓

**Tick when you have:**

reviewed it after your lesson ☑ ☐ ☐

revised once – some questions right ☑ ☑ ☐

revised twice – all questions right ☑ ☑ ☑

*Move on to another topic when you have all three ticks*

| | ✓ | ✓ | ✓ |
|---|---|---|---|
| Nuclear fission | ☐ | ☐ | ☐ |
| Nuclear fusion | ☐ | ☐ | ☐ |
| Nuclear issues | ☐ | ☐ | ☐ |
| The early universe | ☐ | ☐ | ☐ |
| The life history of a star | ☐ | ☐ | ☐ |
| How the chemical elements formed | ☐ | ☐ | ☐ |

**1** A student sets up the series circuit shown in the diagram.

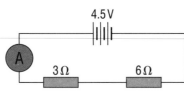

4.5 V

A

3 Ω          6 Ω

**a** What is the reading on the ammeter in amperes? Write down the equation you use. Show clearly how you work out your answer and give the unit. *(4 marks)*

**b** What is the current through
   **i** the 3 Ω resistor *(1 mark)*
   **ii** the 6 Ω resistor? *(1 mark)*

**c** What is the potential difference across
   **i** the 3 Ω resistor *(1 mark)*
   **ii** the 6 Ω resistor? *(1 mark)*

**d** The student wants to connect a voltmeter to the circuit to measure the potential difference across the 6 Ω resistor. Add the correct symbol to the diagram to show how the student should connect the voltmeter. *(2 marks)*

**2** *In this question you will be assessed on using good English, organising information clearly and using specialist terms where appropriate.*

Stars form from clouds of dust and gas. Gravitational forces make the clouds become increasingly dense, forming a protostar.

Describe the life cycle of a star, the size of our Sun, from its beginning as a protostar to its final stage as a black dwarf. Include in your explanation how the star produces energy. *(6 marks)*

**3** A food processor is connected to the 230 V mains supply.
   **a** The power of the food processor is 950 W.
   What is the current through the food processor? Write down the equation you use. Show clearly how you work out your answer and give the unit. *(3 marks)*

   **b** 3 A, 10 A and 13 A fuses are available.
   State and explain what size fuse should be used in the plug for the food processor. *(2 marks)*

   **c** When the food processor is used to make a cake mixture, 738 C of charge flows through the food processor. How long, in minutes, does it take to make the cake mixture? Write down the equation you use. Show clearly how you work out your answer and give the unit. *(4 marks)*

**4** A car starts from rest and is driven along a straight, level road. The graph shows how the velocity of the car changes with time for the first 20 s of its journey.

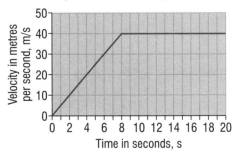

**a** Use the graph to calculate the acceleration of the car during the first 8 s. Show clearly how you work out your answer and give the unit. *(3 marks)*

**b** Use the graph to calculate how far the car travels during the first 20 s of its journey. Show clearly how you work out your answer and give the unit. *(3 marks)*

**c** The car has a mass of 1100 kg.

Calculate the kinetic energy of the car 20 s after it starts its journey. Write down the equation you use. Show clearly how you work out your answer and give the unit. *(3 marks)*

**5** A skydiver jumps from a plane. The skydiver is shown in the diagram.

**a** Arrows X and Y represent two forces acting on the skydiver as she falls through the air. Force Y is the weight of the skydiver.

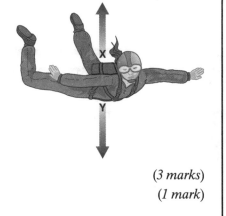

   **i** The mass of the skydiver is 70 kg. Calculate the weight of the skydiver. Write down the equation you use. Show clearly how you work out your answer and give the unit. *(3 marks)*

   **ii** What causes force X? *(1 mark)*

**b** The graph shows how the velocity of the skydiver varies with time as the skydiver falls.

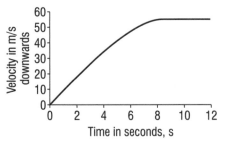

Explain, with reference to the sizes of the forces X and Y, how the velocity of the skydiver varies with time between

   **i** 0 and 8 seconds *(3 marks)*

   **ii** 8 and 12 seconds. *(3 marks)*

# Medical applications of physics

## 1.1 X-rays

Student Book
pages 208–209

### Key points

- X-rays are used in hospitals:
  - to make images and CT scans
  - to destroy tumours at or near the body surface.
- X-rays can damage living tissue when they pass through it.
- X-rays are absorbed more by bones and teeth than by soft tissue.

### Bump up your grade

Remember that X-rays can cause cancer but they can also be used to treat cancer.

**Key words:** X-ray, charge-coupled device (CCD), CT scanner

- **X-rays** are part of the electromagnetic spectrum. They have a high frequency and a very short wavelength. (Their wavelength is about the same size as the diameter of an atom.)
- Properties of X-rays include:
  - they affect a photographic film in the same way as light
  - they are absorbed by metal and bone
  - they are transmitted by healthy tissue.
- X-rays are used to form images of bones on photographic film to check for fractures and dental problems.
- **Charge-coupled devices (CCDs)** can be used to form electronic images of X-rays. **CT scanners** use X-rays to produce digital images of a cross-section through the body. Some body organs made of soft tissue, such as the intestines, can be filled with a contrast medium that absorbs X-rays so that they can be seen on an X-ray image.
- X-rays cause ionisation and can damage living tissue when they pass through it, therefore precautions must be taken when using them. Workers should wear film badges and when possible use lead screens to shield them from the X-rays.
- X-rays may also be used for therapy. They can be used to treat cancerous tumours at or near the body surface.

> **1** *Why do workers in X-ray departments wear lead aprons?*

## 1.2 Ultrasound

### Key points

- Ultrasound waves are sound waves of frequency above 20000 Hz.
- Ultrasound can be used for diagnosis and treatment.
- Ultrasound waves are partly reflected at a boundary between two different types of body tissue.
- An ultrasound scan is non-ionising so it is safer than an X-ray.

### AQA Examiner's tip

You may be asked to do calculations using data from oscilloscope traces.

**Key word:** ultrasound wave

- The human ear can detect sound waves with frequencies between 20 Hz and 20000 Hz. Sound waves of a higher frequency than this are called **ultrasound waves**.
- Electronic systems can be used to produce ultrasound waves. When a wave meets a boundary between two different materials, part of the wave is reflected. The wave travels back through the material to a detector. The time it takes to reach the detector can be used to calculate how far away the boundary is. The results may be processed by a computer to give an image.

> **1** *What is the minimum frequency of an ultrasound wave?*

- The distance travelled by an ultrasound pulse can be calculated using the equation
$$s = v \times t$$
Where:
$s$ is the distance travelled in metres, m
$v$ is the speed of the ultrasound wave in metres per second, m/s
$t$ is the time taken in seconds, s.
- In the time between a transmitter sending out a pulse of ultrasound and it returning to a detector, it has travelled from the transmitter to a boundary and back, i.e. twice the distance to the boundary.
- Ultrasound can be used in medicine for scanning. It is non-ionising, so is safer to use than X-rays. It can be used for scanning unborn babies and soft tissue such as the eye. Ultrasound may also be used in therapy, for example to shatter kidney stones into small pieces.

# 1.3 Refractive index

## Key points

- Refractive index, *n*, is a measure of how much a substance can refract a light ray.

- $n = \dfrac{\sin i}{\sin r}$

### AQA  Examiner's tip

Remember that angles *i* and *r* are measured between the ray and the normal.

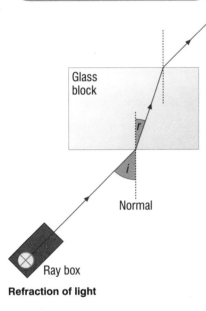

Glass block

Normal

Ray box

**Refraction of light**

- **Refraction** is the change of direction of light as it passes from one transparent substance into another.
- Refraction takes place because waves change speed when they cross a boundary. The change in speed of the waves causes a change in direction, unless the waves are travelling along a normal.

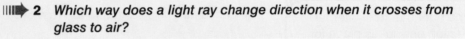 **1   What is refraction?**

- A light ray will refract when it crosses from air into glass. It is refracted towards the normal.
- The **refractive index** of a substance is a measure of how much the substance can refract a light ray.
- The refractive index is given by the equation:

$$n = \frac{\sin i}{\sin r}$$

Where:
*n* is the refractive index of the substance
sin *i* is the sine of the angle of incidence
sin *r* is the sine of the angle of refraction.

**2   Which way does a light ray change direction when it crosses from glass to air?**

### Maths skills

A ray of light travels from air into glass. The angle of incidence is 45° and the angle of refraction is 28°.

Calculate the refractive index of the glass.

$$n = \frac{\sin i}{\sin r}$$

$$n = \frac{\sin 45°}{\sin 28°}$$

$$n = \frac{0.71}{0.47}$$

$$n = 1.5$$

Refractive index is a ratio, so it does not have a unit.

### Bump up your grade

A ray of light travelling along a normal is not refracted.

**Key words:** refraction, refractive index

# 1.4 The endoscope

## Key points

- The critical angle is the angle of incidence of a light ray in a transparent substance which produces refraction along the boundary.

- $n = \dfrac{1}{\sin c}$ [H]

- Total internal reflection occurs when the angle of incidence of a light ray in a transparent substance is greater than the critical angle.

- An endoscope is used to see inside the body directly.

- A light ray will refract when it crosses from glass to air. It is refracted away from the normal. A partially reflected ray is also seen. If the angle of incidence in the glass is gradually increased, the angle of refraction increases until the refracted ray emerges along the boundary. This angle of incidence is called the **critical angle**, c.

- If the angle of incidence is increased beyond the critical angle the light ray undergoes **total internal reflection**. When total internal reflection occurs, the angle of reflection is equal to the angle of incidence.

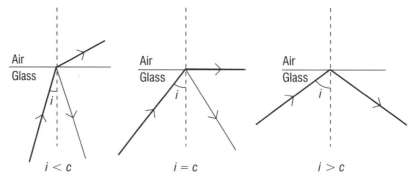

$$i < c \qquad\qquad i = c \qquad\qquad i > c$$

**Refraction and total internal reflection**

## AQA Examiner's tip

Remember that total internal reflection only takes place for a ray travelling from a more dense to a less dense material, e.g. from glass into air.

The critical angle is related to the refractive index by the equation:

$$n = \frac{1}{\sin c}$$

Where:
n is the refractive index
c is the critical angle.

▨▶ **1** *What is the critical angle for glass of refractive index 1.5?*

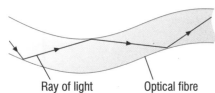

Ray of light    Optical fibre

**Light rays in an optical fibre**

- An **endoscope** is a device used to look inside a patient's body without cutting it open or when performing keyhole surgery. The endoscope contains bundles of **optical fibres**. These are very thin, flexible glass fibres. Visible light can be sent along the fibres by total internal reflection.

- Laser light may be used as an energy source in an endoscope to carry out some surgical procedures such as cutting, cauterising and burning. The colour of the laser light is matched to the type of tissue to produce maximum absorption. Eye surgery on the retina in the eye can be carried out by using laser light that passes straight through the cornea at the front of the eye but is absorbed by the retina at the back.

▨▶ **2** *What is an optical fibre?*

**Key words:** critical angle, total internal reflection, endoscope, optical fibre

# 1.5 Lenses

## Key points

- A converging lens focuses parallel rays to a point called the principal focus.

- A diverging lens makes parallel rays spread out as if they came from a point called the principal focus.

- A real image is formed by a converging lens if the object is further away than the principal focus.

- A virtual image is formed by a diverging lens, and by a converging lens if the object is nearer to the lens than the principal focus.

- Magnification = $\dfrac{\text{image height}}{\text{object height}}$

### AQA Examiner's tip

Make sure you don't confuse the terms 'converging' and 'diverging'.

## Converging (convex) lens

- Parallel rays of light that pass through a **converging (convex) lens** are refracted so that they converge to a point. This point is called the **principal focus** (focal point). The distance from the centre of the lens to the principal focus is the **focal length**.

- Because light can pass through the lens in either direction, there is a principal focus on either side of the lens.

- If the object is further away from the lens than the principal focus, an inverted, **real image** is formed. The size of the image depends on the position of the object. The nearer the object is to the lens, the larger the image.

- If the object is nearer to the lens than the principal focus, an upright, **virtual image** is formed behind the object. The image is magnified – the lens acts as a **magnifying glass**.

- The **magnification** can be calculated using:

$$\text{magnification} = \frac{\text{image height}}{\text{object height}}$$

## Diverging (concave) lens

- Parallel rays of light that pass through a **diverging (concave) lens** are refracted so that they diverge away from a point. This point is called the principal focus.

- The distance from the centre of the lens to the principal focus is the focal length.

- Because light can pass through the lens in either direction, there is a principal focus on either side of the lens.

- The image produced by a diverging (concave) lens is always virtual.

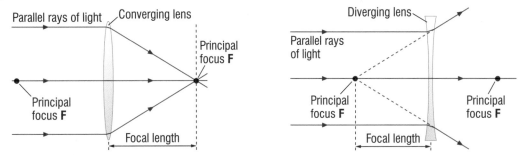

The focal length of a converging lens          The focal length of a diverging lens

 

> **1** What is the principal focus of a converging (convex) lens?
>
> **2** How can a converging lens be made to produce a virtual image?

- The symbols below can be used in ray diagrams to represent lenses.

Converging lens          Diverging lens

**Key words:** converging lens, principal focus, focal length, real image, virtual image, magnifying glass, magnification, diverging lens

# 1.6 Using lenses

## Key points

- A ray diagram can be drawn to find the position and nature of an image formed by a lens.

- When an object is placed between a converging lens and F, the image formed is virtual, upright, magnified and on the same side of the lens as the object.

- A camera contains a converging lens that is used to form a real image of an object.

- A magnifying glass is a converging lens that is used to form a virtual image of an object.

- We can draw ray diagrams to find the image that different lenses produce with objects in different positions.

- The line through the centre of the lens and at right angles to it is called the **principal axis**. Include this in your diagram.

- Ray diagrams use three construction rays from a single point on the object to locate the corresponding point on the image:
  - A ray parallel to the principal axis is refracted through the principal focus.
  - A ray through the centre of the lens travels straight on, without refraction.
  - A ray through the principal focus is refracted parallel to the principal axis.

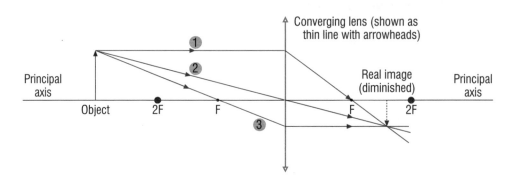

Ray ① is parallel to the axis and is refracted through F
Ray ② passes straight through the centre of the lens
Ray ③ passes through F and is refracted parallel to the axis

**Formation of a real image by a converging lens**

> **1** *What are construction rays?*

- A camera uses a converging lens to form a real image of an object on a film or an array of CCDs.

> **2** *Is the image formed in a camera real or virtual?*

### Bump up your grade

Make sure you practise drawing ray diagrams. Only two of the construction rays are needed to find the image, but if you have time it is worth drawing all three to be sure that you have the correct position.

**Key word:** principal axis

Student Book
pages 220–221

**P3**

# 1.7 The eye

## Key points

- Light is focused on to the retina by the cornea and the eye lens, which is a variable focus lens.

- The normal human eye has a range of vision from 25 cm to infinity.

- $P = \dfrac{1}{f}$

 **Examiner's tip**

When calculating the power of a lens, make sure that the focal length is in metres so that the power of the lens is in dioptres.

## Inside the eye

- Light enters the eye through the **cornea**. The cornea and the **eye lens** focus the light on to the **retina**. The **iris** adjusts the size of the **pupil** to control the amount of light entering the eye.

- The **ciliary muscles** alter the thickness of the lens to control the fine focusing of the eye. They are attached to the lens by the **suspensory ligaments**.

Eye lens – focuses light onto the retina

Iris – coloured ring of muscle that controls the amount of light entering the eye

Cornea – transparent layer that protects the eye and helps to focus light onto retina

Pupil – the central hole formed by the iris. Light enters the eye through the pupil

Ciliary muscles – attached to the lens by suspensory ligaments. The muscles change the thickness of the eye lens

Retina – the light-sensitive cells around the inside of the eye

Blind spot – region where the retina is not sensitive to light (no light-sensitive cells present)

Optic nerve – carries nerve impulses from the retina to the brain

**The human eye**

▶ **1** *Which two structures focus the light entering the eye?*

- The normal human eye has a **near point** of 25 cm and a **far point** of infinity, so its **range of vision** is from 25 cm to infinity.

## Lens power

- The **power of a lens** is given by:

$$P = \frac{1}{f}$$

Where:
$P$ is the power of the lens in **dioptres**, D
$f$ is the focal length of the lens in metres, m.

▶ **2** *What is the power of a lens of focal length 0.25 m?*

**Key words:** near point, far point, range of vision, power of a lens, dioptre

# 1.8  More about the eye

- A person with **short sight** can see close objects clearly, but distant objects are blurred because the uncorrected image is formed in front of the retina. Short sight is caused by the eyeball being too long or the eye lens being too powerful. Short sight may be corrected using a diverging lens.

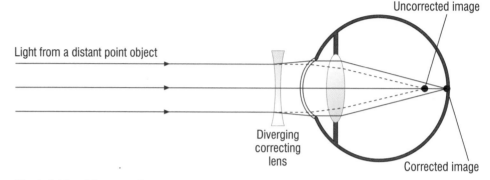

Light from a distant point object

Uncorrected image

Diverging correcting lens

Corrected image

**Short sight and its correction**

**1**  *Which type of lens may be used to correct short sight?*

- A person with **long sight** can see distance objects clearly, but close objects are blurred because the uncorrected image is formed behind the retina. Long sight is caused by the eyeball being too short or the eye lens being too weak. Long sight may be corrected using a converging lens.

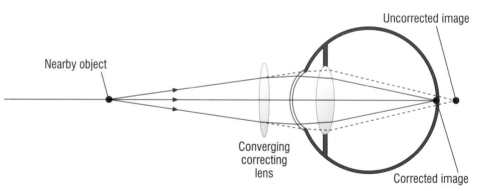

Nearby object

Uncorrected image

Converging correcting lens

Corrected image

**Long sight and its correction**

- The focal length of a lens is determined by:
  - the refractive index of the material from which the lens is made
  - the curvature of the two surfaces of the lens.

For a lens of a given focal length, the greater the refractive index of the lens material, the flatter and thinner the lens can be manufactured.

*Higher*

**2**  *What defect of the eyeball may cause it to be long-sighted?*

**Key words:** short sight, long sight

**1** Why do workers in hospital X-ray departments wear film badges?

**2** What is a CT scanner?

**3** What is an ultrasound wave?

**4** Why are X-rays not normally used to produce an image of an unborn baby?

**5** A ray of light travels through glass of refractive index 1.54. The angle of incidence is 15°. What is the angle of refraction? [H]

**6** What happens to a ray of light that enters a glass block along a normal?

**7** A ray of light strikes the boundary between glass and air at the critical angle. What will happen to the ray?

**8** What is the principal focus of a diverging lens?

**9** Describe the image formed by a diverging lens.

**10** What are the ciliary muscles?

**11** What is the power of a lens of focal length 16 cm?

**12** A lens used as a magnifying glass produces a magnification of 6. If the height of the image is 9 cm, what is the height of the object?

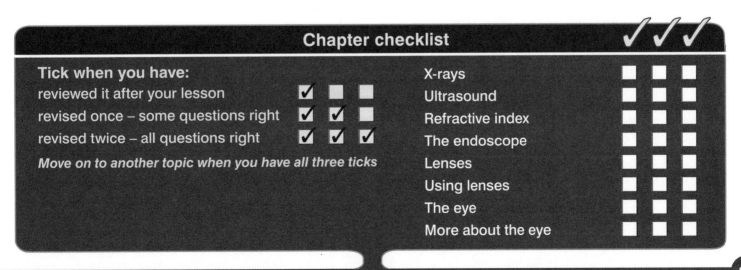

| Chapter checklist | ✓ | ✓ | ✓ |
|---|---|---|---|
| **Tick when you have:** | | | |
| reviewed it after your lesson | ✓ | ☐ | ☐ |
| revised once – some questions right | ✓ | ✓ | ☐ |
| revised twice – all questions right | ✓ | ✓ | ✓ |
| *Move on to another topic when you have all three ticks* | | | |

| | | | |
|---|---|---|---|
| X-rays | ☐ | ☐ | ☐ |
| Ultrasound | ☐ | ☐ | ☐ |
| Refractive index | ☐ | ☐ | ☐ |
| The endoscope | ☐ | ☐ | ☐ |
| Lenses | ☐ | ☐ | ☐ |
| Using lenses | ☐ | ☐ | ☐ |
| The eye | ☐ | ☐ | ☐ |
| More about the eye | ☐ | ☐ | ☐ |

Student Book
pages 226–227 **P3**

## 2.1 Moments

- The turning effect of a force is called its **moment**.
- The size of the moment is given by the equation:

$$M = F \times d$$

Where:
$M$ is the moment of the force in newton-metres, Nm
$F$ is the force in newtons, N
$d$ is the perpendicular distance from the **line of action** of the force to the **pivot** in metres, m.

> **1** *A door opens when you apply a force of 20 N at right angles to it, 0.6 m from the hinge. What is the moment of the force about the hinge?*
>
> **2** *What force would be needed to open the door if it were applied 0.3 m from the hinge?*
> [H]

- To increase the moment:
  - either the force must increase
  - or the distance to the pivot must increase.
- It is easier to undo a wheel-nut by pushing on the end of a long spanner than a short one. That's because the long spanner increases the distance between the line of action of the force and the pivot.
- We make use of a lever to make a job easier. When using a lever, the force we are trying to move is called the **load** and the force applied to the lever is the **effort**. A lever acts as a force multiplier, so the effort we apply can be much less than the load.

### Key points

- The moment of a force is a measure of the turning effect of the force on an object.
- $M = F \times d$
- To increase the moment of a force $F$, increase $F$ or increase $d$.

**A turning effect**

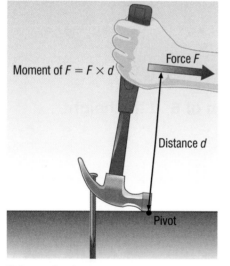

Moment of $F = F \times d$

Force $F$

Distance $d$

Pivot

**Using a claw hammer**

### AQA Examiner's tip

In examination questions, moments may be applied to lots of different situations such as:
- opening a door or a can of paint
- moving something heavy in a wheelbarrow, or
- using a crowbar or a spanner.

The idea is always the same; for any particular force, make the distance to the pivot bigger to make the moment bigger.

### Bump up your grade

Notice that the moment equation uses the term 'perpendicular distance'. This means the shortest distance from the line that the force acts along.

**Key words:** moment, line of action, pivot, load, effort

## 2.2 Centre of mass

- Although any object is made up of many particles, its mass can be thought of as being concentrated at one single point. This point is called the **centre of mass**.
- Any object that is freely suspended will come to rest with its centre of mass directly below the point of suspension. The object is then in **equilibrium**.

> **1** *What is the centre of mass of an object?*

- You can find the centre of mass of a thin irregular sheet of a material as follows:
  - Suspend the thin sheet from a pin held in a clamp stand. Because it is freely suspended, it is able to turn.
  - When it comes to rest, hang a plumbline from the same pin.
  - Mark the position of the plumbline against the sheet.
  - Hang the sheet with the pin at another point and repeat the procedure.
  - The centre of mass is where the lines that marked the position of the plumbline cross.
- The position of the centre of mass depends on the shape of the object, and sometimes lies outside the object.
- For a symmetrical object, its centre of mass is along the axis of symmetry. If the object has more than one axis of symmetry, the centre of mass is where the axes of symmetry meet.

> **2** *Where is the centre of mass of a symmetrical object?*

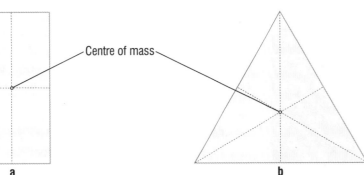

Centre of mass

a

b

**Symmetrical objects**

### Key points

- The centre of mass of an object is that point where its mass can be thought to be concentrated.
- When a suspended object is in equilibrium, its centre of mass is directly beneath the point of suspension.
- The centre of mass of a symmetrical object is along the axis of symmetry.

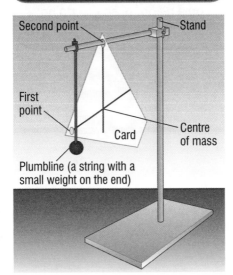

Second point
Stand
First point
Card
Centre of mass
Plumbline (a string with a small weight on the end)

**Finding the centre of mass of a card**

### AQA Examiner's tip

Make sure that you can describe the experiment to find the centre of mass of a thin sheet of a material, including sketching a labelled diagram.

**Key words:** centre of mass, equilibrium

Student Book
pages 230–231 **P3**

# 2.3 Moments in balance

- If an object is in equilibrium it is balanced, not turning. We can take the moments about *any* point and will find that the total clockwise moment and the total anticlockwise moment are equal.
- There are lots of everyday examples of the **principle of moments**, such as seesaws and balance scales.

> **1** If someone sits in the centre of a seesaw, the moment about the pivot is zero. Why?
>
> **2** Aimie sits 2m from the centre of a seesaw. Leo weighs twice as much as Aimie. How far from the centre must he sit to balance the seesaw? **[H]**

### Bump up your grade

Be sure to add together all the clockwise moments and all the anticlockwise moments. It may help to tick them off if they are on a diagram, so you do not miss any out. **[H]**

**Key word:** principle of moments

---

Student Book
pages 232–233 **P3**

# 2.4 Stability

- The line of action of the weight of an object acts through its centre of mass.

If the line of action of the weight lies outside the base of an object, there will be a **resultant moment** and the object will tend to topple over.

> **1** Why does hanging heavy bags from the handle of a pushchair make it more likely to topple over?

- The wider the base of an object, and the lower its centre of mass, the further it has to tilt before the line of action of the weight moves outside the base. So the stability of an object is increased by making its base wider and its centre of mass lower.

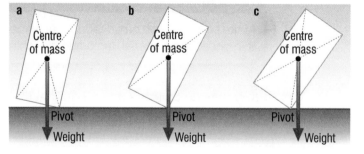

Tilting and toppling **a** tilted, **b** at balance, **c** toppled over

> **2** Why do ten-pin bowling pins have a narrow base and a high centre of gravity?

**Key word:** resultant moment

# 2.5 Hydraulics

- **Pressure** is given by the equation:

$$P = \frac{F}{A}$$

Where:
$P$ is the pressure in pascals, Pa (or N/m²)
$F$ is the force in newtons, N
$A$ is the cross-sectional area at right angles to the direction of the force in metres squared, m².

▶ **1** *What is the pressure exerted on the ground by a person of weight 300 N if the area of their feet in contact with the ground is 0.04 m²?*

- Liquids are virtually incompressible and the pressure in a liquid is transmitted equally in all directions. This means that a force exerted at one point on a liquid will be transmitted to other points in the liquid. This is made use of in **hydraulic pressure** systems.

- The force exerted by a hydraulic pressure system depends on:
  - the force exerted on the system
  - the area of the cylinder on which this force acts on
  - the area of the cylinder that exerts the force.

- The use of different cross-sectional areas on the effort and load sides of a hydraulic system means that the system can be used as a **force multiplier**. Therefore, a small effort can be used to move a large load.

### Maths skills

In a hydraulic pressure system, a force of 25 N is applied to a piston of area 0.50 m². The area of the other piston is 1.5 m². Calculate the pressure transmitted through the system and the force exerted on the other piston.

$$P = \frac{F}{A}$$

$$P = \frac{25\,N}{0.5\,m^2}$$

$$P = 50\,Pa$$

Pressure transmitted is 50 Pa.

$F = P \times A$

$F = 50\,Pa \times 1.5\,m^2$

$F = 75\,N$

Force exerted on the other piston is 75 N.

▶ **2** *What properties of a liquid make it useful in a hydraulic system?*

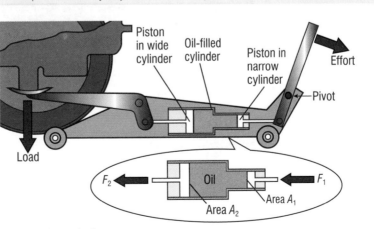

A hydraulic car jack

## Key points

- $P = \frac{F}{A}$

- The pressure in a fluid acts equally in all directions.

- A hydraulic system uses the pressure in a fluid to exert a force.

 **Examiner's tip**

Remember that a hydraulic pressure system is usually used as a force multiplier. So if you calculate that the force produced by such a system is less than the effort applied to the system you have made a mistake.

**Key words:** pressure, hydraulic pressure

# 2.6 Circular motion

- The velocity of an object moving in a circle at constant speed is continually changing as the object's direction is continually changing.

- Centripetal acceleration is the acceleration towards the centre of the circle of an object that is moving round the circle.

- The centripetal force on an object depends on its mass, its speed and the radius of the circle.

- When an object moves in a circle it is continuously changing direction, so it is continuously changing velocity. In other words, it is accelerating. This acceleration is called the **centripetal acceleration**.

- An object only accelerates when a resultant force acts on it. This force is called the **centripetal force** and always acts towards the centre of the circle.

- If the centripetal force stops acting, the object will continue to move in a straight line at a tangent to the circle.

- The centripetal force needed to make an object perform circular motion increases as:
  - the mass of the object increases
  - the speed of the object increases
  - the radius of the circle decreases.

**Whirling an object around**

> **1** *A student is whirling a conker around on a piece of string, in a horizontal circle. What force provides the centripetal force?*
>
> **2** *What will happen to the conker if the string breaks?*

## AQA Examiner's tip

Centripetal force is not a force in its own right. It is always provided by another force, for example gravitational force, electric force or tension.

In questions on circular motion, you may need to identify the force that provides the centripetal force.

**Key words:** centripetal acceleration, centripetal force

Student Book
pages 238–239

**P3**

# 2.7 The pendulum

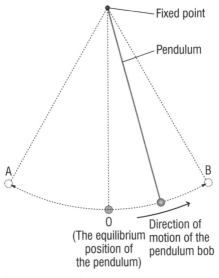

Fixed point

Pendulum

A

B

0
(The equilibrium position of the pendulum)

Direction of motion of the pendulum bob

**The pendulum**

- A pendulum moves to and fro along the same line. This is an example of **oscillating motion**.

- A **simple pendulum** consists of a mass, called a bob, suspended on the end of a string. When the bob is displaced to one side and let go, the pendulum oscillates back and forth, through the equilibrium position. (The equilibrium position is the position of the pendulum when it stops moving).

- The **amplitude** of the oscillation is the distance from the equilibrium position to the highest position on either side.

- The **time period** of the oscillation is the time taken for one complete cycle, this is:
  - the time taken from the highest position on one side to the highest position on the other side and back to the start position, or
  - the time taken between successive passes in the same direction through the equilibrium position.
  To measure the time period of a pendulum, we can measure the average time for 20 oscillations and divide the timing by 20.

- The time period depends only on the length of the pendulum and increases as its length increases.

- The frequency of the oscillations is the number of complete cycles of oscillation per second.

- The time period and frequency are related by the equation:

$$T = \frac{1}{f}$$

Where:
$T$ is the time period in seconds, s
$f$ is the frequency in hertz, Hz.

### Maths skills

What is the time period of a pendulum that completes 20 oscillations in 5.0 seconds?

There are $\frac{20.0}{5.0} = 4.0$ oscillations in 1 second, so the frequency is 4.0 Hz.

$$T = \frac{1}{f}$$

$$T = \frac{1}{4.0 \, Hz}$$

$$T = 0.25 \, s$$

The time period is 0.25 seconds.

- A playground swing is an example of an oscillating motion. If not pushed repeatedly, the swing will come to rest. This is because energy is transferred due to friction at the top of the swing and due to air resistance.

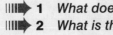 **1** *What does the time period of a simple pendulum depend on?*
 **2** *What is the time period of a pendulum of frequency 10 Hz?*

**Key words:** oscillating motion, simple pendulum, amplitude, time period

**1** What is the moment of a force?

**2** Why is it easier to move a big rock with a crowbar than with your hands?

**3** Where is the position of the centre of mass of each of the shapes below?

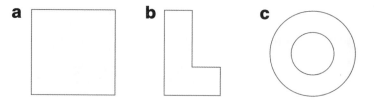

a   b   c

**4** Why must an object moving in a circle be accelerating?

**5** A force of 15 N is applied at right angles to the end of a spanner 0.5 m long. What is the moment of this force?

**6** An object that is freely suspended is displaced slightly then let go. Where will its centre of mass be when it comes to rest?

**7** What is the pressure exerted on the ground by a block of weight 20 N if the area in contact with the ground is 0.008 m²?

**8** What is a centripetal acceleration?

**9** Why will an oscillating simple pendulum eventually come to rest?

**10** What is the frequency of a pendulum with a time period of 0.02 s?

**11** What is the amplitude of oscillation of a simple pendulum?

**12** When will an object topple?

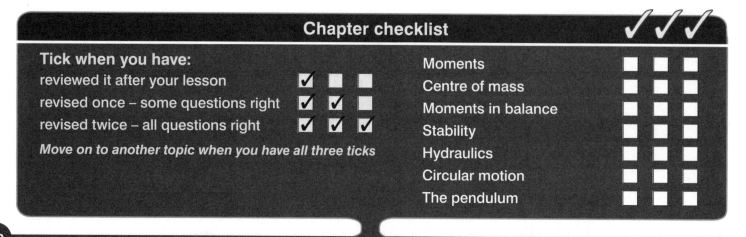

**Chapter checklist**

**Tick when you have:**
reviewed it after your lesson
revised once – some questions right
revised twice – all questions right
*Move on to another topic when you have all three ticks*

Moments
Centre of mass
Moments in balance
Stability
Hydraulics
Circular motion
The pendulum

Student Book
pages 242–243

**P3**

# 3.1 Electromagnets

## Key points

- The force between two magnets: like poles repel; unlike poles attract.

- A magnetic field line is the line along which a plotting compass points.

- An electromagnet consists of a coil of insulated wire wrapped round an iron core.

- Electromagnets are used in scrapyard cranes, circuit breakers, electric bells and relays.

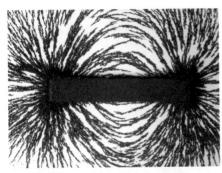

**The magnetic field near a bar magnet**

## About magnets

- The ends of a magnet are called **magnetic poles**. There is a **north pole** at one end and a **south pole** at the other. The region around the magnet, in which a piece of iron or steel will be attracted to it, is called its **magnetic field**. Iron filings placed near a magnet will form a pattern of lines that loop from one pole to the other. These are **lines of force** or magnetic **field lines**. A plotting compass placed in the magnetic field will always point along a field line.

- If two magnets are brought close to each other with like poles together (north and north or south and south) they will repel each other.

- If unlike poles are together (north and south or south and north) they will attract each other.

▐▌▐▶ **1** *What is a magnetic field?*

## Electromagnets

- When a current flows through a wire, a magnetic field is produced around the wire. An electromagnet is made by wrapping insulated wire around a piece of iron, called the core. When a current flows through the wire the iron becomes strongly magnetised. When the current is switched off the iron loses its magnetism. This temporary magnetism makes electromagnets very useful.

- Electromagnets are used in devices such as scrapyard cranes, circuit breakers, electric bells and relays.

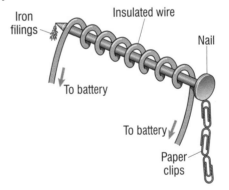

**A simple electromagnet**

▐▌▐▶ **2** *What does an electromagnet consist of?*

AQA **Examiner's tip**

In the exam you may be given a diagram of an appliance that contains an electromagnet and asked to explain how it works.

**Key words:** magnetic pole, north pole, south pole, line of force, field line

# 3.2 The motor effect

## Key points

- In the motor effect, the force:
  - is increased if the current or the strength of the magnetic field is increased,
  - is at right angles to both the direction of the magnetic field and to the wire,
  - is reversed if the direction of either the current or the magnetic field is reversed.
- An electric motor has a coil which turns when a current is passed through it.

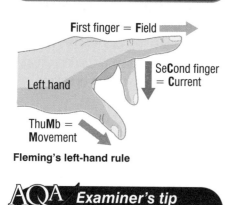

First finger = **F**ield

Left hand

Se**C**ond finger = **C**urrent

Thu**M**b = **M**ovement

**Fleming's left-hand rule**

- When we place a wire carrying an electric current in a magnetic field, it may experience a force. This is called the **motor effect**.
- The force is a maximum if the wire is at an angle of 90° to the magnetic field, and zero if the wire is parallel to the magnetic field.
- Fleming's left-hand rule is used to determine the direction of the force. The thumb and first two fingers of the left hand are all held at right angles to each other:
  - the first finger represents the magnetic field (pointing north to south)
  - the second finger represents the current (pointing positive to negative)
  - the thumb represents the direction of the force.
- The size of the force can be increased by:
  - increasing the strength of the magnetic field
  - increasing the size of the current.
- The direction of the force on the wire is reversed if either the direction of the current or the direction of the magnetic field is reversed.
- The motor effect is used in different appliances.

> **1** *What happens to the direction of the force on a wire carrying a current if the direction of the current and the magnetic field are both reversed?*

## The electric motor

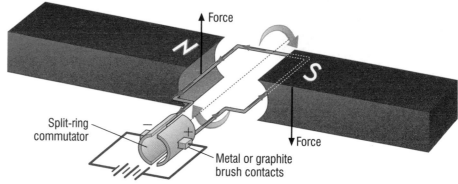

**The electric motor**

- The diagram shows a simple electric motor.
  - The speed of the motor is increased by increasing the size of the current.
  - The direction of the motor can be reversed by reversing the direction of the current.
- When a current passes through the coil, the coil spins because:
  - a force acts on each side of the coil due to the motor effect
  - the force on one side of the coil is in the opposite direction to the force on the other side.
- The **'split-ring' commutator** reverses the direction of the current around the coil every half-turn. Because the sides swap over each half-turn, the coil is always pushed in the same direction.

> **2** *The ends of the coil in a motor are parallel to the magnetic field. What is the size of the force on them?*

---

**Key words:** motor effect, split-ring commutator

Student Book
pages 246–247

**P3**

# 3.3 Electromagnetic induction

- If an electrical conductor 'cuts' through magnetic field lines, a potential difference (pd) is induced across the ends of the conductor.

- If a magnet is moved into a coil of wire, a pd is induced across the ends of the coil. This process is called **electromagnetic induction**. If the wire or coil is part of a complete circuit, a current passes through it.

## Key points

- Electromagnetic induction is the process of creating a potential difference using a magnetic field.

- When a conductor cuts the lines of a magnetic field, a potential difference is induced across the ends of the conductor.

- When an electromagnet is used, it needs to be switched on or off to induce a pd.

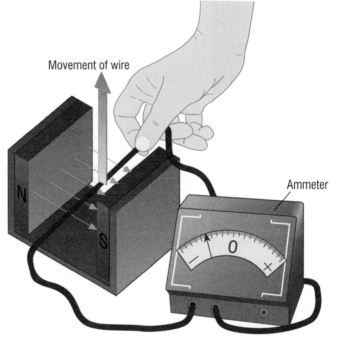

**Electromagnetic induction**

- If the direction of movement of the wire or coil is reversed, or the polarity of the magnet is reversed, the direction of the induced pd is also reversed. A pd is only induced while there is movement.

> **1** *Why is there no potential difference induced when a bar magnet is held stationary inside a coil of wire?*

- The size of the induced pd is increased by increasing:
    - the speed of movement
    - the strength of the magnetic field
    - the number of turns on the coil.

> **2** *What is the effect on the induced pd of reversing the direction of the current in a conductor cutting magnetic field lines?*

## Bump up your grade

Remember a potential difference is induced only when the wire or coil and the magnetic field move relative to each other.

**Key word:** electromagnetic induction

# 3.4 Transformers

- A **transformer** consists of two coils of insulated wire, called the primary coil and the secondary coil. These coils are wound on to the same iron core. When an alternating current passes through the primary coil, it produces an alternating magnetic field in the core. This field continually expands and collapses.

- The alternating magnetic field lines pass through the secondary coil and induce an alternating potential difference across its ends. If the secondary coil is part of a complete circuit an alternating current is produced.

- The coils of wire are insulated so that current does not short across either the iron core or adjacent turns of wire, but flows around the whole coil. The core is made of iron so it is easily magnetised.

- Transformers are used in the **National Grid**.
  - A **step-up transformer** makes the pd across the secondary coil greater than the pd across the primary coil. Its secondary coil has more turns than its primary coil.
  - A **step-down transformer** makes the pd across the secondary coil less than the pd across the primary coil. Its secondary coil has fewer turns than its primary coil.

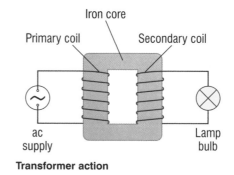

**Transformer action**

> **1** *Why is the core of a transformer made of iron not copper?*

- A **switch mode transformer** has a ferrite core. Compared with a traditional transformer, a switch mode transformer:
  - operates at a much higher frequency
  - is lighter and smaller
  - uses very little power when there is no device connected across its output terminals.

> **2** *What happens if a 1.5 V cell is used as the supply for the primary coil?*

**AQA Examiner's tip**

Remember there is no current in the iron core, just a magnetic field.

**Key words:** transformer, National Grid, step-up transformer, step-down transformer, switch mode transformer

## Key points

- A transformer only works on ac because a changing magnetic field is necessary to induce ac in the secondary coil.

- A transformer has an iron core unless it is a switch mode transformer which has a ferrite core.

- A switch mode transformer is lighter and smaller than an ordinary transformer. It operates at high frequency.

### Bump up your grade

Transformers do not work with dc, but only ac. If a dc passes through the primary coil a magnetic field is produced in the core, but it would not be continually expanding and collapsing, so no pd would be induced in the secondary coil.

Student Book pages 250–251 P3

# 3.5 Transformers in action

## Key points

- Transformers are used to step potential differences up or down.
- $\frac{V_p}{V_s} = \frac{n_p}{n_s}$
- For a step-down transformer, $n_s$ is less than $n_p$
- For a step-up transformer, $n_s$ is greater than $n_p$.
- For a 100% efficient transformer:

  $V_p \times I_p = V_s \times I_s$

## Maths skills

A step-up transformer is used to change a pd of 12 V to a pd of 120 V. If there are 50 turns on the primary coil, how many turns are there on the secondary coil?

$V_p = 12\,V$

$V_s = 120\,V$

$n_p = 50$

$$\frac{V_p}{V_s} = \frac{n_p}{n_s}$$

$$n_s = \frac{n_p V_s}{V_p}$$

$$n_s = \frac{50 \times 120\,V}{12\,V}$$

$$n_s = 500$$

There are 500 turns on the secondary coil.

- The National Grid uses transformers to step-up the pd from power stations.
- This is because the higher the pd at which electrical energy is transmitted across the Grid, the smaller the energy wasted in the cables.
- Step-down transformers are used to reduce the pd so that it is safe to be used by consumers.
- The pd across, and the number of turns on, the primary and secondary coils are related by the equation:

$$\frac{V_p}{V_s} = \frac{n_p}{n_s}$$

Where:

$V_p$ is the pd across the primary coil in volts, V

$V_s$ is the pd across the secondary coil in volts, V

$n_p$ is the number of turns on the primary coil

$n_s$ is the number of turns on the secondary coil.

- A step-down transformer has less turns on the secondary coil than on the primary coil.
- A step-up transformer has more turns on the secondary coil than on the primary coil.

**1** *Why is a transformer used to step-up the pd from a power station?*

- Transformers are almost 100% efficient. For 100% efficiency:

$$V_p \times I_p = V_s \times I_s$$

Where:

$I_p$ is the current in the primary in amperes, A,

$I_s$ is the current in the secondary in amperes, A.

**2** *A transformer has 100 turns on the primary coil and 400 turns on the secondary coil. The pd across the primary coil is 2 V. What is the pd across the secondary coil?*

## Bump up your grade

Make sure you can rearrange the transformer equation.

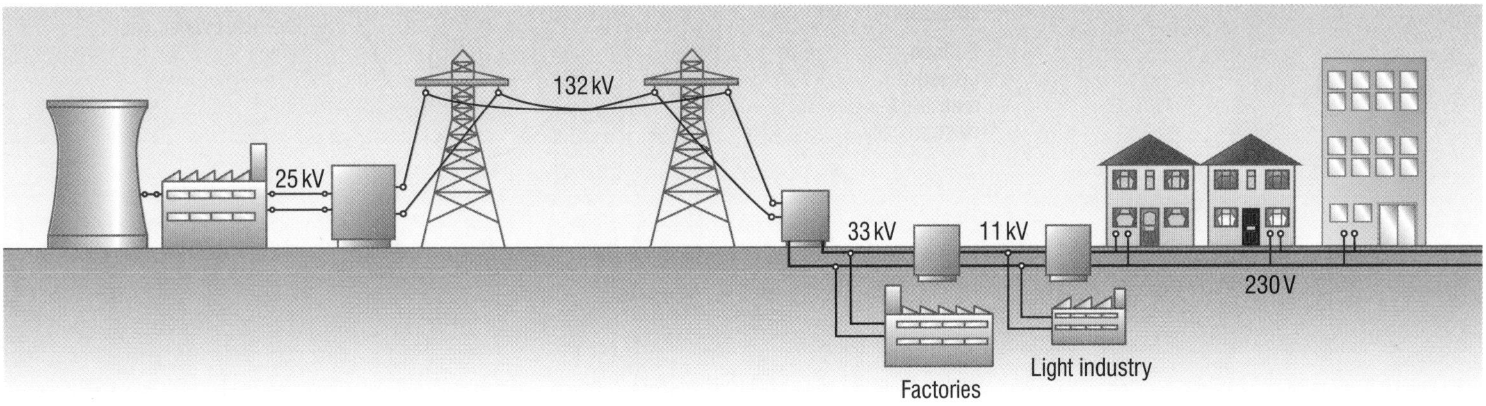
25 kV
132 kV
33 kV
11 kV
230 V
Factories
Light industry

**The grid system**

# 3.6  A physics case study

- We use physics in hospitals whenever:
  - blood pressure (or temperature) is measured
  - an ECG recording is used
  - an endoscope is used
  - a scanner is used.
- We measure blood pressure, ECG potential differences and exposure to ionising radiation in hospitals.
- A CT scanner uses X-rays which are ionising radiation and can therefore damage living tissue.

- Applications of physics are used in hospitals for both diagnosis and therapy.
- An ECG or electrocardiogram is used to measure the potential differences generated by the heart.
- Electronic devices are used to measure the blood pressure.
- Digital thermometers are used to measure temperature.
- An endoscope containing bundles of fibre optics is used to look inside the body without making large incisions.
- X-rays are used to take pictures of suspected broken bones.
- CT scanners are used to build up digital pictures of a cross-section through the body.
- MR scanners use radio waves to produce detailed digital pictures of the body.

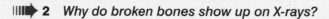 **1**  *Which part of the electromagnetic spectrum is used in a CT scanner?*

**AQA**  *Examiner's tip*

In the exam you will be expected to apply your physics knowledge to unfamiliar situations.

**2**  *Why do broken bones show up on X-rays?*

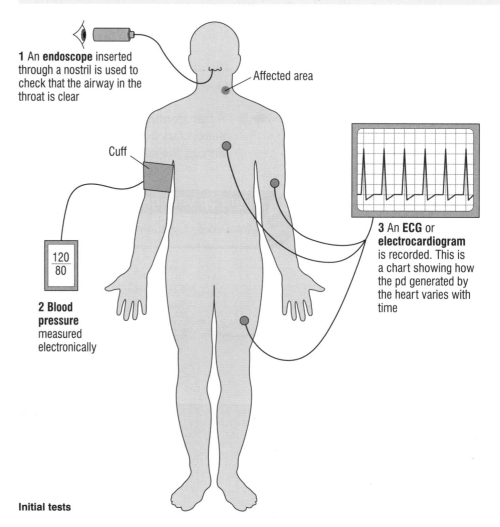

**1** An **endoscope** inserted through a nostril is used to check that the airway in the throat is clear

Affected area

Cuff

120
80

**2 Blood pressure** measured electronically

**3** An **ECG** or **electrocardiogram** is recorded. This is a chart showing how the pd generated by the heart varies with time

Initial tests

**1** Why must insulated wire be used to make an electromagnet?

**2** What is a magnetic field line?

**3** What does the thumb represent in Fleming's left-hand rule?

**4** How can the size of the force in a motor be increased?

**5** What happens if a magnet is held at rest in a coil and the coil is pulled off it?

**6** How can the size of an induced pd be increased?

**7** What does a transformer consist of?

**8** How does the frequency of operation of a switch mode transformer compare with a traditional transformer?

**9** Where is a step-down transformer used in the National Grid?

**10** A transformer is used to step-down a 240 V supply to 12 V. There are 100 turns on the primary coil. How many turns are there on the secondary coil?

**11** A transformer is used to step-down a 240 V supply to 12 V. If the current in the primary coil is 0.1 A, what is the current in the secondary coil?

**12** What is the core of a switch mode transformer made from?

| Chapter checklist | ✓ | ✓ | ✓ |
|---|---|---|---|
| **Tick when you have:** | | | |
| reviewed it after your lesson ✓ ☐ ☐ | Electromagnets | ☐ ☐ ☐ |
| revised once – some questions right ✓ ✓ ☐ | The motor effect | ☐ ☐ ☐ |
| revised twice – all questions right ✓ ✓ ✓ | Electromagnetic induction | ☐ ☐ ☐ |
| *Move on to another topic when you have all three ticks* | Transformers | ☐ ☐ ☐ |
| | Transformers in action | ☐ ☐ ☐ |
| | A physics case study | ☐ ☐ ☐ |

**1** The diagram shows a seesaw. The centre of mass of the seesaw is at its centre.

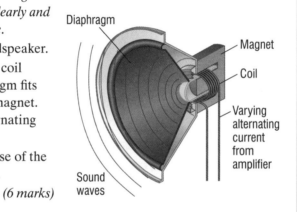

**a** What is meant by 'centre of mass of the seesaw'? *(1 mark)*

**b** A child of weight 460 N sits 2.0 m from the pivot. A second child sits on the other side of the pivot and the seesaw becomes balanced.

  **i** Why must the second child sit on the other side of the pivot? *(2 marks)*

  **ii** The weight of the second child is 575 N. How far away from the pivot must the second child sit for the seesaw to become balanced?

    Show clearly how you work out your answer and give the unit. *(4 marks)*

**c** Explain what would happen if the children were to sit one at each end of the seesaw. *(2 marks)*

**AQA Examiner's tip**

**Qu 1bii** There are four marks for this calculation. Make sure that you show your working step by step so that if you make a mistake you may still get some credit.

**2** *In this question you will be assessed on using good English, organising information clearly and using specialist terms where appropriate.*

The diagram shows a moving coil loudspeaker. The loudspeaker contains a moveable coil attached to a diaphragm. The diaphragm fits loosely over a cylindrical permanent magnet. An amplifier produces a varying, alternating current in the coil.

Explain how the loudspeaker makes use of the motor effect to produce a sound wave. *(6 marks)*

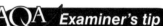

**AQA Examiner's tip**

There are six marks available for this question. To gain all of them your explanation must be in a logical order. Before you write anything stop and think about the points you want to make and the order you want to put them in.

**3** The diagram shows a human eye.

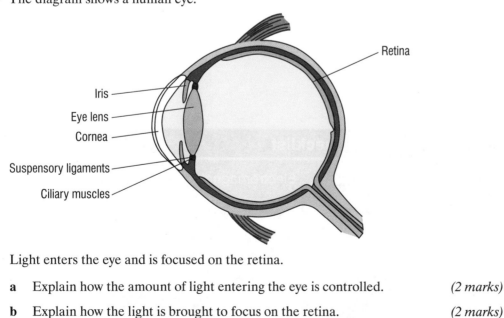

Light enters the eye and is focused on the retina.

**a** Explain how the amount of light entering the eye is controlled. *(2 marks)*

**b** Explain how the light is brought to focus on the retina. *(2 marks)*

**4** The diagram shows the basic structure of a step-down transformer.

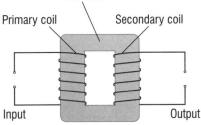

Iron core

Primary coil    Secondary coil

Input    Output

**a** Explain how the transformer works. *(5 marks)*

**b** The transformer is used to change the 230 V mains supply to a 12 V supply to operate a model train.

   **i** There are 30 turns on the secondary coil. Calculate the number of turns on the primary coil.

     Write down the equation you use and show clearly how you work out your answer. *(3 marks)*

   **ii** The current drawn from the mains electricity supply by the transformer is 0.048 A. Calculate the current through the model train.

     Assume that the transformer is 100% efficient.

     Write down the equation you use. Show clearly how you work out your answer and give the unit. *(2 marks)*

**5** A doctor wants to look inside a patient's stomach, without operating on him.

**a** The doctor uses an endoscope. The endoscope contains bundles of optical fibres. Explain how visible light and bundles of optical fibres are used in the endoscope to look inside the patient's stomach. *(3 marks)*

**b** The tube below the stomach is called the small intestine. The doctor wants to take an X-ray picture of the small intestine. Before the picture is taken, the patient is given a drink containing barium, a substance that absorbs X-rays.

   **i** Explain why a normal X-ray will not allow the doctor to see the small intestine. *(2 marks)*

   **ii** Explain why giving the patient barium allows the doctor to see the small intestine on an X-ray picture. *(2 marks)*

   **iii** During this procedure the radiographer stands behind a lead screen. Explain why the radiographer needs to stand behind a lead screen but the patient does not. *(4 marks)*

**AQA** *Examiner's tip*

Remember that it is the magnetic field that passes through the iron core of the transformer, not current or pd.

**AQA** *Examiner's tip*

Make sure that your explanation includes a mention of critical angle and total internal reflection.

# Answers

## P1 Answers

### 1 Energy transfer by heating

#### 1.1
1 The higher the temperature of an object the greater the rate at which it emits infrared radiation.
2 A vacuum is a region that doesn't contain anything at all, even gas particles.

#### 1.2
1 Houses in hot countries are often painted white because white is the worst absorber of infrared radiation.
2 The pipes on the back of a fridge are usually painted black because black surfaces are the best emitters of infrared radiation.

#### 1.3
1 The particles in a liquid are in contact with each other but are not held in fixed positions like those in a solid.
2 The particles in a gas are much farther apart and move around much faster than those in a liquid.

#### 1.4
1 The metal base of the saucepan is a good conductor so heat is conducted quickly to the food in the pan. The wooden handle is a poor conductor so it prevents someone picking up the saucepan getting burnt.
2 Air is a poor conductor so materials that trap air are good insulators.

#### 1.5
1 Convection does not occur in solids because the particles are held in fixed positions and not able to flow.
2 A fluid becomes less dense when heated because it expands, so there is the same mass of material in a larger volume.

#### 1.6
1 Decreasing the surface area of a liquid would decrease the rate of evaporation.
2 Decreasing the surface area would decrease the rate of condensation.

#### 1.7
1 Painting an object dull black maximises the rate of energy transfer, because dull black surfaces are the best emitters of radiation.
2 Trapping air in small pockets minimises the rate of energy transfer because convection currents cannot be set up.

#### 1.8
1 The energy needed is 2100 J.
2 The energy needed is 8400 J.

#### 1.9
1 Fibreglass is a good insulator because it contains trapped air.
2 The pipes that contain the water in a solar heating panel are often painted black because black is the best absorber of radiation.

### Answers to end of chapter questions
1 Dull black
2 All the particles are held together in fixed positions.
3 The most energetic molecules leave the liquid, so the average kinetic energy of the remaining molecules is reduced.
4 If the temperature difference is reduced, the rate of energy transfer decreases.
5 Conduction, convection and evaporation involve particles.

6 Energy from the Sun reaches the Earth as radiation that travels through space.
7 The colour of a surface has no effect on the rate of conduction.
8 Gases are poor conductors because the particles are far apart.
9 Metals are the best conductors because they contain free electrons.
10 Convection is the movement of energy through a fluid by movement of the fluid itself.
11 Cavity wall insulation traps the air in the cavity in pockets, so preventing convection currents from being set up.
12 The energy needed is 50 400 J.

### 2 Using energy

#### 2.1
1 Elastic potential energy
2 From the food that you eat

#### 2.2
1 Chemical to electrical to light and transfer by heating
2 Chemical energy in the fuel is transferred to the surroundings, which get warmer.

#### 2.3
1 It is transferred to the surroundings which get warmer.
2 Because the law of conservation tells us that energy cannot be destroyed

#### 2.4
1 The efficiency is 0.2 or 20%.
2 The efficiency increases.

### Answers to end of chapter questions
1 Kinetic energy
2 Elastic potential energy
3 When an electric current flows
4 Electrical energy to kinetic energy and energy transferred by heating
5 Electrical energy to light and sound
6 Kinetic energy to gravitational potential energy to kinetic energy
7 Its efficiency decreases.
8 Efficiency of the motor is ¾ or 0.75 or 75%.
9 Because it is designed to transfer energy by heating, which is normally how appliances waste energy
10 So that wasted energy can be transferred easily to the surroundings making them warmer, rather than the television or computer
11 42 J
12 750 000 J

### 3 Electrical energy

#### 3.1
1 Electrical energy to kinetic energy
2 A television/computer

#### 3.2
1 12 000 W
2 400 W

#### 3.3
1 2.25 kWh
2 2.16p

#### 3.4
1 The removal or disposal of old equipment and environmental taxes
2 7.5 years

### Answers to end of chapter questions
1 Electrical to energy heating bread
2 As light from the glowing filament
3 Heating the body of the kettle itself, and possibly sound
4 30 kW
5 A 2.2 kW hairdryer
6 Energy is measured in kilojoules.
7 100 W
8 1 kWh
9 The joule is too small to be useful in this situation.
10 40%
11 60p
12 11p            [H]

### 4 Generating electricity

#### 4.1
1 Coal, oil and gas
2 Nuclear fission

#### 4.2
1 Gravitational potential energy
2 There are always two tides a day (tides depend on gravitational pull of the Sun and Moon), but on a calm day there may not be many waves (waves depend on winds, which are unreliable) [or equivalent answer].

#### 4.3
1 Each solar cell only produces a small amount of electricity.
2 In many places in the world the hot rocks are too far below the surface to be used.

#### 4.4
1 A large, flat area of high ground
2 A renewable energy source is produced as fast as it is used. A non-renewable energy source is one that is used at a much faster rate than it is produced.
3 Sulfur dioxide

#### 4.5
1 Overhead cables are easier to repair and are cheaper.
2 A step-down transformer

#### 4.6
1 The demand increases in winter because it gets colder so more electricity is used heating homes.
2 Gravitational potential energy

### Answers to end of chapter questions
1 E.g. methane from waste, ethanol from fermented sugar cane, nutshells
2 The water must fall from a height to transfer gravitational potential energy to kinetic energy.
3 Energy can be obtained from falling water, waves and the tides.
4 A fossil fuel is a fuel that is obtained from long-dead biological materials: coal, oil or gas.
5 Heat in rocks deep below the Earth's surface
6 In portable devices that only require small amounts of electricity, such as watches and calculators. In sunny places that are not connected to a grid system, such as remote villages in hot countries.
7 A solar cell is a device that produces electricity directly from energy from the Sun.
8 A solar heating panel is a device that heats water using energy from the Sun.

9 Non-renewable energy resources are the most reliable.
10 They emit $CO_2$ that can cause global warming and $SO_2$ that can cause acid rain.
11 The pipes are usually painted black.
12 Geothermal energy is renewable, free and does not produce polluting gases.

## 5 Waves

### 5.1
1 They are pushed closer together.
2 Transverse, mechanical waves

### 5.2
1 10 m/s
2 Hertz, Hz

### 5.3
1 A line drawn perpendicular to a reflecting surface
2 The same size as the object

### 5.4
1 Because waves change speed when they cross a boundary
2 Because different wavelengths of light are refracted by different amounts

### 5.5
1 Because the wavelength of light is very short
2 All waves are diffracted.

### 5.6
1 20 Hz to 20 000 Hz (20 kHz)
2 An echo

### 5.7
1 The pitch decreases.
2 The waveforms are different.

### Answers to end of chapter questions

1 The metre, m
2 A virtual, upright image, same size as the object
3 1.5 m behind the mirror
4 Violet
5 The reflection of a sound
6 The region in a longitudinal wave where the particles are further apart than in the rest position
7 Their speed changes
8 The spreading of a wave as it passes through a gap or around an obstacle
9 The air in the flute vibrates as you blow across the mouthpiece.
10 The frequency of the sound wave
11 3.3 m/s
12 20 Hz    [H]

## 6 Electromagnetic waves

### 6.1
1 Hertz, Hz
2 Gamma rays

### 6.2
1 Radio waves

### 6.3
1 By applying an alternating voltage to an aerial

### 6.4
1 The observed wavelength increases.
2 The most distant ones
3 The furthest galaxies are moving the fastest so everything is expanding outwards.

### 6.5
1 The theory that the universe began with a massive explosion from a small initial point.
2 The wavelength increases.

### Answers to end of chapter questions

1 Radio waves
2 Ultraviolet
3 1 000 000 Hz
4 Radio waves
5 Microwaves
6 By total internal reflection
7 The apparent change in wavelength and frequency of waves from a moving source
8 A very large collection of stars
9 It has been shifted towards the red end of the spectrum.
10 By observing the position of dark lines in the spectrum from the galaxy
11 It has become stretched out to microwave wavelengths.
12 The existence of cosmic microwave background radiation

### Answers to examination-style questions

1 a Conduction    (1 mark)
  b The water at the bottom expands as it is heated and becomes less dense. This warmer water rise upwards and is replaced by cooler water at the bottom. This water is also heated and rises, setting up a convection current.    (4 marks)
  c $E = m \times c \times \theta$
    $E = 1.2 \times 4200 \times 80$
    $E = 403200 J$    (3 marks)
  d Some of the energy is wasted heating the body of the kettle. This energy spreads into the surroundings, making them warmer.    (3 marks)

2 Marks awarded for this answer will be determined by the Quality of Written Communication (QWC) as well as the standard of the scientific response.

There is a clear and detailed description of how the kinetic theory explains the properties of solids, liquids and gases. The answer shows almost faultless spelling, punctuation and grammar. It is coherent and in an organised, logical sequence. It contains a range of appropriate or relevant specialist terms used accurately.    (5–6 marks)
There is a description of how the kinetic theory explains the properties of solids, liquids and gases. There are some errors in spelling, punctuation and grammar. The answer has some structure and organisation. The use of specialist terms has been attempted, but not always accurately.    (3–4 marks)
There is a brief description of how the kinetic theory explains the properties of solids, liquids and gases, which has little clarity and detail. The spelling, punctuation and grammar are very weak. The answer is poorly organised with almost no specialist terms and/or their use demonstrating a general lack of understanding of their meaning.    (1–2 marks)
No relevant content.    (0 marks)

**Examples of physics points made in the response:**
• particles in a solid are held next to each other in fixed positions
• they vibrate about these positions, so a solid has a fixed shape and volume
• in a liquid, particles are in contact with each other so liquid has a fixed volume
• the particles move about at random, so a liquid has no fixed shape and can flow
• particles in a gas are much farther apart than in a liquid and move much faster
• so gas has no fixed shape or volume.

3 a i Electrical to kinetic    (1 mark)
    ii Transferred to the surroundings, which become warmer    (1 mark)
  b i Useful energy transferred = 1000 – 300 = 700 J    (1 mark)
    ii Percentage efficiency
       $= \dfrac{\text{useful energy out}}{\text{total energy in}} \times 100\%$
       $= \dfrac{700}{1000} \times 100$
       $= 70\%$    (3 marks)
  c Energy = power × time or $E = p \times t$
    Power = 800 W = 0.8 kW, time $= \dfrac{15}{60}$
    = 0.25 hours
    Energy = 0.8 × 0.25 = 0.2 kWh
    Cost = 0.2 × 12 = 2.4p    (4 marks)
4 a A non-renewable energy source    (1 mark)
  b The energy is used to heat water which becomes steam and turns a turbine that drives a generator.    (4 marks)
  c i Nuclear energy is reliable; only a small amount of fuel is needed to produce a large amount of energy.    (2 marks)
    ii A nuclear power station produces nuclear waste that is radioactive for a long time and must be stored or disposed of safely. Nuclear fuels are costly, but the energy from wind is free once the set-up cost has been paid.    (2 marks)
5 a The back of the mirror is where reflection takes place.    (1 mark)
  b i A virtual image cannot be formed on a screen, because the rays of light that produce the image only appear to pass through it.    (2 marks)
    ii The image is: 4 cm tall, upright, 6 cm behind the back of the mirror.    (3 marks)
  c Real rays correct
    Virtual rays correct
    Image position correct    (3 marks)
6 a The sound wave makes the particles of air vibrate.
    The wave is longitudinal so the vibrations are perpendicular to the direction of travel of the wave.
    The wave travels as a series of compressions and rarefactions.    (3 marks)
  b i Trace has same shape
       Same frequency
       Bigger amplitude    (3 marks)
    ii Trace has same shape
       Higher frequency
       Same amplitude    (3 marks)

# P2 Answers

## 1 Motion

### 1.1
1 Metres, m
2 8 m/s

### 1.2
1 Velocity is speed in a particular direction.
2 metres per second squared, m/s²

### 1.3
1 Constant velocity, zero acceleration
2 A straight line with a negative gradient

### 1.4
1 a Increasing velocity
  b Increasing acceleration

### Answers to end of chapter questions

1 20 m/s
2 Straight horizontal line

3 Acceleration
4 A deceleration
5 The gradient increases.
6 By changing its direction.
7 4 m/s$^2$
8 Area between the line and the x-axis
9 10 m/s
10 20 m/s
11 1 m/s$^2$ [H]
12 50 m [H]

## 2 Forces

**▶ 2.1**
1 Newton, N
2 Downwards (or towards (the centre of) the Earth)

**▶ 2.2**
1 Newton, N
2 7 N in the same direction as the two forces

**▶ 2.3**
1 Acceleration decreases
2 2000 N

**▶ 2.4**
1 Zero
2 Stopping distance = thinking distance + braking distance

**▶ 2.5**
1 There is a resultant force acting on it.
2 It will reach a terminal velocity because the resultant force becomes zero.

**▶ 2.6**
1 An inelastic object is one that does **not** regain its original shape when the forces deforming it are removed.
2 9 N
3 The graph of extension against force applied is no longer a straight line.

**▶ 2.7**
1 Less engine force and less power are needed to maintain a certain speed. Less fuel is needed so fuel costs are reduced.
2 The vehicle is not accelerating, so the resultant force on it is zero. So the engine force and air resistance are balanced.

## Answers to end of chapter questions

1 15 N to the left
2 The object continues to move at a steady speed in the same direction.
3 When the force is in the opposite direction to the motion.
4 The acceleration increases.
5 750 N
6 0.4 m/s$^2$
7 The faster the speed the greater the stopping distance.
8 The final steady speed of an object falling freely through a fluid.
9 700 N
10 One that goes back to its original size and shape when the force applied to it is removed.
11 The extension is directly proportional to the force applied, provided the limit of proportionality is not exceeded.
12 500 N/m

## 3 Work, energy and momentum

**▶ 3.1**
1 Joule, J
2 2400 J

**▶ 3.2**
1 320 J
2 160 W

**▶ 3.3**
1 500 J
2 Some elastic potential energy is transferred by heating.

**▶ 3.4**
1 When they are moving
2 30 000 kg m/s

**▶ 3.5**
1 The total momentum before the explosion
2 It is equal and opposite.

**▶ 3.6**
1 Time taken for a collision to take place
2 Cars may be hit from either the front or the rear, in either case the crumple zone reduces the forces on the car (or increases the impact time).

**▶ 3.7**
1 a They continue to move forwards when the car stops and will hit the windscreen.
  b The narrow seatbelt would not spread the force across the passenger's body and might cut them.

## Answers to end of chapter questions

1 When a force moves through a distance
2 Work done = energy transferred
3 Watt, W
4 54 J
5 The energy stored in an elastic object when it is stretched or squashed
6 540 000 J
7 kg m/s or Ns
8 50 000 kg m/s
9 The thick foam mat increases the impact time compared with the hard floor, reducing the force on the gymnast.
10 2.0 m [H]
11 1.3 s [H]
12 0.6 m/s to the right [H]

## 4 Current electricity

**▶ 4.1**
1 It gains electrons.
2 They will repel each other.

**▶ 4.2**
1
2

**▶ 4.3**
1 An ammeter
2 Ohm, Ω

**▶ 4.4**
1 The resistance of the LDR increases.
2 Reversing the pd has no effect on the current–potential difference curve for the filament bulb.

**▶ 4.5**
1 There is no complete path for the current, so no current flows.
2 Add all the individual resistances.

**▶ 4.6**
1 Current cannot flow through that component but it can flow in other parts of the circuit.
2 They are equal.

## Answers to end of chapter questions

1 Negative
2 It loses electrons.
3 A repulsive force
4

5 60 Ω
6 4.5 V
7 A conductor that obeys Ohm's law – the current is directly proportional to resistance if the temperature is constant.
8 The resistance in one direction is very high, so there is no current. In the opposite direction the resistance is lower so current will flow.
9 The potential difference across it increases.
10 13 Ω
11 The ammeter should be placed in series and the voltmeter in parallel with the resistor.
12 0.75 A

## 5 Mains electricity

**▶ 5.1**
1 Current that passes in one direction only
2 0 V

**▶ 5.2**
1 Brass is a good conductor and does not rust or oxidise.
2 So that the case cannot become live and electrocute you

**▶ 5.3**
1 A thin wire that heats up and melts if too much current passes through it
2 Plastic is an insulator so it cannot become live.

**▶ 5.4**
1 3 kW
2 2300 W

**▶ 5.5**
1 240 C
2 46 000 J [H]

**▶ 5.6**
1 The case of the hairdryer is plastic, so it doesn't need an earth.
2 They transfer a lot of energy by heating, rather than as light.

## Answers to end of chapter questions

1 230 V
2 50 Hz
3 +/– 325 V
4 Blue
5 It has green and yellow stripes.
6 Plastic is a good electrical insulator.
7 3 A
8 Coulomb, C
9 An electromagnetic switch that opens and cuts off the supply if the current is bigger than a certain value.
10 30 000 J
11 10 A
12 12 V [H]

## 6 Radioactivity

**▶ 6.1**
1 The nucleus
2 It stays the same.

**▶ 6.2**
1 Most of the atom is empty space.
2 The nucleus is where most of the mass of the atom is concentrated, very small and positively charged.

**▶ 6.3**
1 +2
2 –1

**▶ 6.4**
1 Alpha
2 Gamma

## ➤ 6.5
1 It decreases.
2 It has decreased to one quarter of its original value.

## ➤ 6.6
1 Alpha particles are very poorly penetrating, so they would not be detected outside the body/ Alpha is very ionising so would be damaging to the patient.
2 To allow time to complete the procedure but minimise unnecessary exposure of the patient.

## Answers to end of chapter questions
1 It has no effect.
2 Radiation that is around us all the time.
3 Firing alpha particles at a thin metal foil
4 It stays the same.
5 It goes up by 1.
6 It goes down by 4.
7 It goes down by 2.
8 Gamma radiation is uncharged.
9 It has decreased to one-eighth of its original value.
10 Alpha radiation would not be able to pass through the foil, irrespective of thickness.
11 3 milligrams
12 12 500

### 7 Energy from the nucleus

## ➤ 7.1
1 Uranium that contains 2–3% uranium-235
2 A nucleus absorbs a neutron.

## ➤ 7.2
1 Fusion
2 In a magnetic field

## ➤ 7.3
1 Radon gas
2 So that it does not enter the environment because it remains radioactive

## ➤ 7.4
1 It decreased.
2 A collection of billions of stars held together by their own gravity

## ➤ 7.5
1 The forces acting on them are balanced.
2 The core left after a supernova explodes

## ➤ 7.6
1 Iron
2 By a supernova explosion

## Answers to end of chapter questions
1 An isotope that can undergo the process of fission
2 Uranium-235 and plutonium-239
3 When each fission event causes further fission events
4 The process of forcing two nuclei close enough together so they form a single larger nucleus.
5 Nuclear fusion can be brought about by making two light nuclei collide at very high speed.
6 Millions of years
7 Not even light can escape from it.
8 After a supernova, if the star has sufficient mass
9 A black dwarf
10 The presence of the heavier elements in the Sun and inner planets
11 Fusion
12 In a supernova

### Answers to examination-style questions

1 a $R = 3\,\Omega + 6\,\Omega = 9\,\Omega$

$I = \dfrac{V}{R}$

$I = 4.5\dfrac{V}{9\,\Omega}$

$I = 0.5\,A$         (4 marks)

  b  i   0.5 A          (1 mark)
      ii   0.5 A          (1 mark)
  c  i   1.5 V          (1 mark)
      ii   3.0 V          (1 mark)
  d  Correct symbol shown in parallel across the 6 Ω resistor      (2 marks)

2 Marks awarded for this answer will be determined by the Quality of Written Communication (QWC) as well as the standard of the scientific response.

There is a clear, balanced and detailed description of the life cycle of a star. The answer shows almost faultless spelling, punctuation and grammar. It is coherent and in an organised, logical sequence. It contains a range of appropriate or relevant specialist terms used accurately.        (5–6 marks)
There is a description of the life cycle of a star. There are some errors in spelling, punctuation and grammar. The answer has some structure and organisation. The use of specialist terms has been attempted, but not always accurately.        (3–4 marks)
There is a brief description of the life cycle of a star, which has little clarity and detail. The spelling, punctuation and grammar are very weak. The answer is poorly organised with almost no specialist terms and/or their use demonstrating a general lack of understanding of their meaning.        (1–2 marks)
No relevant content.        (0 marks)

**Examples of physics points made in the response:**
• as the protostar becomes denser, it gets hotter
• the nuclei of hydrogen atoms and other light elements start to fuse together releasing energy in the process
• this stage can continue for billions of years, the star is stable and is called a main sequence star
• eventually the star runs out of hydrogen nuclei
• the star swells, cools down and is now a red giant
• helium and other light elements fuse to form heavier elements
• fusion stops and the star will contract to form a white dwarf
• eventually no more light is emitted and the star becomes a black dwarf.

3 a $I = \dfrac{P}{V}$

$I = \dfrac{950\,W}{230\,V}$

$= 4.1\,A$        (3 marks)

  b  Should use 10 A.
3 A too low and would blow as soon as processor switched on, 13 A too big to protect the appliance.        (2 marks)

  c  $I = \dfrac{Q}{t}$

$t = \dfrac{Q}{I}$

$= \dfrac{738}{4.1}$

$= 180\,s$

$= \dfrac{180}{60} = 3$ minutes      (4 marks)

4 a Acceleration = gradient

$a = \dfrac{40}{8}$

$= 5.0\,m/s^2$        (3 marks)

  b  Distance travelled = area under graph
$s = (0.5 \times 8 \times 40) + (12 \times 40) = 160 + 480$
$= 640\,m$        (3 marks)

  c  $E_k = \frac{1}{2} \times m \times v^2$
At 20 s, speed = 40 m/s
$E_k = \frac{1}{2} \times 1100\,kg \times (40\,m/s)^2$
$E_k = 880\,000\,J$        (3 marks)

5 a i  $W = m \times g$
$W = 70\,kg \times 10\,N/kg$
$W = 700\,N$        (3 marks)
   ii  Air resistance        (1 mark)

  b  i  Initially X is 0 so the only downward force is Y, so the skydiver accelerates downwards.
Gradient = acceleration, so initial gradient is steepest.
As velocity increases X increases, so acceleration decreases so gradient of line becomes less steep up to $t = 8\,s$.        (3 marks)

     ii  At 8 seconds X and Y are equal, so the resultant force is 0, so the acceleration is 0, skydiver travels at terminal velocity, so graph is a horizontal straight line.        (3 marks))

# P3 Answers

### 1 Medical applications of physics

## ➤ 1.1
1 To shield them, the lead absorbs X-rays.

## ➤ 1.2
1 20 000 Hz

## ➤ 1.3
1 The change in direction of a wave as it crosses from one transparent material to another.
2 It refracts away from the normal.

## ➤ 1.4
1 42°                            [H]
2 A very thin, flexible glass fibre

## ➤ 1.5
1 The point where rays of light parallel to the principal axis are brought to a focus
2 By placing an object between the lens and the principal focus

## ➤ 1.6
1 Rays drawn on a diagram to determine the position and nature of an image
2 Real

## ➤ 1.7
1 Cornea and lens
2 4.0 d

## ➤ 1.8
1 A diverging lens
2 The eyeball is too short, or eye lens too weak.

## Answers to end of chapter questions
1 To monitor their exposure to X-rays
2 A device that uses X-rays to produce digital images of a cross-section through the body
3 A sound wave with a frequency greater than the upper limit for human hearing, i.e. 20 000 Hz
4 X-rays are ionising, so might harm the baby.
5 9.7°                            [H]
6 It passes into the block without changing direction.

7 It will be refracted at an angle of 90°, along the boundary between the glass and the air.

8 The point that parallel rays of light appear to have diverged from after they have passed through the lens.

9 Virtual, upright, smaller than the object

10 The muscles that control the thickness of the lens in the eye

11 6.25 d

12 1.5 cm

## 2 Using physics to make things work

### ▐▐▐▶ 2.1
1 12 Nm
2 40 N                                                    [H]

### ▐▐▐▶ 2.2
1 The point where the mass of the object can be thought to be concentrated
2 Along the axis of symmetry

### ▐▐▐▶ 2.3
1 Because their perpendicular distance to the pivot is zero
2 1 m                                                      [H]

### ▐▐▐▶ 2.4
1 The bags raise the centre of mass so the pushchair will not have to tilt so far before the line of action of the weight moves outside the base.
2 So they are likely to topple over when hit by a bowling ball

### ▐▐▐▶ 2.5
1 7500 Pa
2 Liquids are virtually incompressible, and the pressure in a liquid is transmitted equally in all directions.

### ▐▐▐▶ 2.6
1 Tension in the string
2 The conker will fly off in a straight line at a tangent to the circle.

### ▐▐▐▶ 2.7
1 The length of the string
2 0.1 s

## Answers to end of chapter questions
1 The turning effect of a force
2 A crowbar allows you to apply the same force at a greater distance from the pivot, giving a bigger moment.
3 a ▢ b ▢ c ⊗

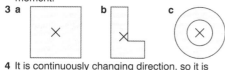

4 It is continuously changing direction, so it is continuously changing velocity.
5 7.5 Nm
6 Directly below the point of suspension
7 2500 Pa
8 An acceleration towards the centre of a circle
9 It transfers energy doing work against friction at the pivot and air resistance.
10 50 Hz
11 The distance from the highest point on one side of the oscillation to the highest point on the other side.
12 When the line of action of its weight is outside its base.

## 3 Using magnetic fields to keep things moving

### ▐▐▐▶ 3.1
1 The region around a magnet, in which a piece of iron or steel will be attracted to it

2 An electromagnet consists of a piece of insulated wire wrapped around an iron core.

### ▐▐▐▶ 3.2
1 It stays the same.
2 Zero

### ▐▐▐▶ 3.3
1 The stationary bar magnet is not cutting any magnetic field lines.
2 The direction of the induced pd is reversed.

### ▐▐▐▶ 3.4
1 Iron can be magnetised.
2 The transformer will not work, as it requires an ac supply. A cell supplies dc.

### ▐▐▐▶ 3.5
1 So that the electrical energy can be transmitted at a high pd, reducing energy wasted in the cables
2 8 V

### ▐▐▐▶ 3.6
1 X-rays
2 X-rays are absorbed by bone.

## Answers to end of chapter questions
1 To stop current short-circuiting between the loops of wire
2 A line along which a plotting compass will point
3 The direction of the force
4 By increasing the strength of the magnetic field or the size of the current
5 A pd is induced across the ends of the coil.
6 By increasing the speed of movement, increasing the strength of the magnetic field, or increasing the number of turns on the coil
7 A transformer consists of two coils of insulated wire wound on an iron core.
8 A switch mode transformer operates at a much higher frequency.
9 In a sub-station before transmission to consumers
10 5
11 2A
12 Ferrite

## Answers to examination-style questions

1 a The point at which the mass of the seesaw may be thought to be concentrated    *(1 mark)*
  b i There is a moment about the pivot from one child. For the seesaw to balance there must be an equal and opposite moment from the other child. The moment will only be opposite if the child sits on the other side of the pivot.    *(2 marks)*
    ii $F_1 \times d_1 = F_2 \times d_2$
       $d_2 = \dfrac{F_1 \times d_1}{F_2}$
       $d_2 = \dfrac{460\,N \times 2.0\,m}{575\,N}$
       $d_2 = 1.6\,m$    *(4 marks)*
  c The second child has a bigger weight than the first. If they are both the same distance from the pivot the moment of the second child is bigger. So his end of the seesaw will go down.    *(2 marks)*
2 Marks awarded for this answer will be determined by the Quality of Written Communication (QWC) as well as the standard of the scientific response.

There is a clear, balanced and detailed explanation of how the loudspeaker makes use of the motor effect to produce a sound wave. The answer shows almost faultless spelling, punctuation and grammar. It is coherent and in an organised, logical sequence. It contains a range of appropriate or relevant specialist terms used accurately.    *(5–6 marks)*

There is a description of how the loudspeaker makes use of the motor effect to produce a sound wave. There are some errors in spelling, punctuation and grammar. The answer has some structure and organisation. The use of specialist terms has been attempted, but not always accurately.    *(3–4 marks)*
There is a brief description of how the loudspeaker makes use of the motor effect to produce a sound wave, which has little clarity and detail. The spelling, punctuation and grammar are very weak. The answer is poorly organised with almost no specialist terms and/or their use demonstrating a general lack of understanding of their meaning.    *(1–2 marks)*
No relevant content.    *(0 marks)*

**Examples of physics points made in the response:**
• a coil that carries a current in a magnetic field experiences a force
• this is called the motor effect
• the current from the amplifier varies so the current in the coil varies and the force varies
• the force makes the coil move
• the coil is attached to the diaphragm so the diaphragm moves
• the diaphragm makes the surrounding air move, producing a sound wave.

3 a The iris is a ring of muscle that controls the size of the pupil and hence the amount of light entering the eye.    *(2 marks)*
  b The light is made to converge by both the cornea and by the eye lens to form an image on the retina.    *(2 marks)*
4 a There must be an alternating input supplied to the primary coil, which causes an alternating magnetic field in the iron core. This field passes through the secondary coil inducing an alternating pd across the secondary coil.    *(5 marks)*
  b i $\dfrac{V_p}{V_s} = \dfrac{n_p}{n_s}$
       $n_p = \dfrac{V_p \times n_s}{V_s}$
       $n_p = \dfrac{230\,V \times 30}{12\,V}$
       $n_p = 575$    *(3 marks)*
    ii $V_p \times I_p = V_s \times I_s$
       $I_s = \dfrac{V_p \times I_p}{V_s}$
       $I_s = \dfrac{230\,V \times 0.048\,A}{12\,V}$
       $I_s = 0.92\,A$    *(2 marks)*
5 a Visible light enters the end of an optical fibre at an angle greater than the critical angle. The light is able to travel down the fibre by total internal reflection. The light is able to follow a curved path. The stomach can be illuminated and an image seen.    *(3 marks)*
  b i The small intestine is made of soft tissue. This does not absorb X-rays so will not show up on an X-ray picture.    *(2 marks)*
    ii Barium absorbs X-rays. So if the small intestine contains barium it will absorb X-rays and hence show up on the picture.    *(2 marks)*
    iii X-rays are ionising so they are damaging to cells.
       The lead screen will absorb X-rays reducing the dose to the radiographer. Unlike the radiographer the patient is not regularly exposed to X-rays and infrequent exposure carries a low risk.    *(4 marks)*

# Glossary

## A

**Absorber** A substance that takes in radiation.

**Acceleration** Change of velocity per second (in metres per second per second, m/s²).

**Alpha radiation** Alpha particles, each composed of two protons and two neutrons, emitted by unstable nuclei.

**Alternating current** Electric current in a circuit that repeatedly reverses its direction.

**Amplitude** The height of a wave crest or a wave trough of a transverse wave from the rest position. Of oscillating motion, is the maximum distance moved by an oscillating object from its equilibrium position.

**Angle of incidence** Angle between the incident ray and the normal.

**Angle of reflection** Angle between the reflected ray and the normal.

**Atomic number** The number of protons (which equals the number of electrons) in an atom. It is sometimes called the proton number.

**Attract** To cause to move nearer.

## B

**Band** Part of the radio and microwave spectrum used for communications.

**Base load** Constant amount of electricity generated by power stations.

**Beta radiation** Beta particles that are high-energy electrons created in and emitted from unstable nuclei.

**Big Bang theory** The theory that the universe was created in a massive explosion (the Big Bang) and that the universe has been expanding ever since.

**Biofuel** Fuel made from animal or plant products.

**Black dwarf** A star that has faded out and gone cold.

**Black hole** An object in space that has so much mass that nothing, not even light, can escape from its gravitational field.

**Blue-shift** Decrease in the wavelength of electromagnetic waves emitted by a star or galaxy due to its motion towards us. The faster the speed of the star or galaxy, the greater the blue-shift is.

**Boundary** Line along which two substances meet.

**Braking distance** The distance travelled by a vehicle during the time its brakes act.

## C

**Cable** Two or three insulated wires surrounded by an outer layer of rubber or flexible plastic.

**Centre of mass** The point where an object's mass may be thought to be concentrated.

**Centripetal acceleration** The acceleration of an object moving in a circle at constant speed. Centripetal acceleration always acts towards the centre of the circle.

**Centripetal force** The resultant force towards the centre of a circle acting on an object moving in a circular path.

**Chain reaction** Reactions in which one reaction causes further reactions, which in turn cause further reactions, etc. A nuclear chain reaction occurs when fission neutrons cause further fission, so more fission neutrons are released. These go on to produce further fission.

**Charge-coupled device (CCD)** Used to record and display an image.

**Chemical energy** Energy of an object due to chemical reactions in it.

**Circuit breaker** An electromagnetic switch that opens and cuts the current off if too much current passes through it.

**Compression** Squeezed together.

**Condensation** Turning from vapour into liquid.

**Conduction** Transfer of energy from particle to particle in matter.

**Conductor** Material/object that conducts.

**Conservation of energy** Energy cannot be created or destroyed.

**Conservation of momentum** In a closed system, the total momentum before an event is equal to the total momentum after the event. Momentum is conserved in any collision or explosion provided no external forces act on the objects that collide or explode.

**Convection** Transfer of energy by the bulk movement of a heated fluid.

**Convection current** The circular motion of matter caused by heating in fluids.

**Converging lens** A lens that makes light rays parallel to the principal axis converge to (i.e. meet at) a point; also referred to as a convex lens.

**Cosmic microwave background radiation** Electromagnetic radiation that has been travelling through space ever since it was created shortly after the Big Bang.

**Cost effectiveness** How much something gives value for money when purchase, running and other costs are taken into account.

**Critical angle** The angle of incidence of a light ray in a transparent substance which produces refraction along the boundary.

**Crumple zone** Region of a vehicle designed to crumple in a collision to reduce the force on the occupants.

**CT scanner** A medical scanner that uses X-rays to produce a digital image of any cross-section through the body or a three-dimensional image of an organ.

## D

**Deceleration** Change of velocity per second when an object slows down.

**Diffraction** The spreading of waves when they pass through a gap or around the edges of an obstacle that has a similar size as the wavelength of the waves.

**Diode** Electrical device that allows current flow in one direction only.

**Dioptre** The unit of lens power, D.

**Direct current** Electric current in a circuit that is in one direction only.

**Directly proportional** A graph will show this if the line of best fit is a straight line through the origin.

**Diverging lens** A lens that makes light rays parallel to the axis diverge (i.e. spread out) as if from a single point; also referred to as a concave lens.

**Doppler effect** The change of wavelength (and frequency) of the waves from a moving source due to the motion of the source towards or away from the observer.

**Drag force** A force opposing the motion of an object due to fluid (e.g. air) flowing past the object as it moves.

## E

**Echo** Reflection of sound that can be heard.

**Efficiency** Useful energy transferred by a device ÷ total energy supplied to the device.

**Effort** The force applied to a device used to raise a weight or shift an object.

**Elastic** A material is elastic if it is able to regain its shape after it has been squashed or stretched.

**Elastic potential energy** Energy stored in an elastic object when work is done to change its shape.

**Electrical appliance** Machine powered by electricity.

**Electrical energy** Energy transferred by the movement of electrical charge.

**Electromagnetic induction** The process of inducing a potential difference in a wire by moving the wire so it cuts across the lines of force of a magnetic field.

**Electromagnetic spectrum** A set of radiations that have different wavelengths and frequencies but all travel at the same speed in a vacuum.

**Electromagnetic wave** Electric and magnetic disturbance that transfers energy from one place to another. The spectrum of electromagnetic waves, in order of increasing wavelength, is as follows: gamma and X-rays, ultraviolet radiation, visible light, infrared radiation, microwaves, radio waves.

**Electron** A tiny particle with a negative charge. Electrons orbit the nucleus in atoms or ions.

**Emit** Give out radiation.

**Emitter** A substance that gives out radiation.

**Endoscope** Optical device used by a surgeon to see inside the body. The device contains two bundles of flexible optical fibres, one used to transmit light into the body and the other used to see inside the body.

**Energy transfer** Movement of energy from one place to another or one form to another.

**Equilibrium** The state of an object when it is at rest.

**Evaporation** Turning from liquid into vapour.

# F

**Far point** The furthest point from an eye at which an object can be seen in focus by the eye. The far point of a normal eye is at infinity.

**Field line** See line of force.

**Filament bulb** Electrical device designed to produce light.

**Fluid** A liquid or a gas.

**Focal length** The distance from the centre of a lens to the point where light rays parallel to the principal axis are focused (or, in the case of a diverging lens, appear to diverge from).

**Force** A force can change the motion of an object (in newtons, N).

**Fossil fuel** Fuel obtained from long-dead biological material.

**Free electron** Electron that moves about freely inside a metal and is not held inside an atom.

**Frequency** The number of wave crests passing a fixed point every second.

**Frequency (of an alternating current)** The number of complete cycles an alternating current passes through each second. The unit of frequency is the hertz (Hz).

**Friction** Force opposing the movement of one surface over another.

**Fuse** A fuse contains a thin wire that melts and cuts the current off if too much current passes through it.

# G

**Gamma radiation** Electromagnetic radiation emitted from unstable nuclei in radioactive substances.

**Gamma ray** The highest energy wave in the electromagnetic spectrum.

**Gas** A state of matter.

**Generator** A machine that produces a voltage.

**Geothermal energy** Energy from hot underground rocks.

**Gravitational attraction** Force that pulls two masses together.

**Gravitational field strength, g** The force of gravity on an object of mass 1 kg (in newtons per kilogram, N/kg).

**Gravitational potential energy** Energy of an object due to its position in a gravitational field. Near the Earth's surface, change of GPE (in joules, J) = weight (in newtons, N) × vertical distance moved (in metres, m).

# H

**Half-life (of a radioactive isotope)** Average time taken for the number of nuclei of the isotope (or mass of the isotope) in a sample to halve.

**Hooke's law** The extension of a spring is directly proportional to the force applied, provided its limit of proportionality is not exceeded.

**Hydraulic pressure** The pressure in the liquid in a hydraulic arm.

# I

**Impact time** Time taken for a collision to take place.

**Infrared radiation** Electromagnetic waves between visible light and microwaves in the electromagnetic spectrum.

**Input energy** Energy supplied to a machine.

**Insulating** Reducing energy transfer by heating.

**Insulator** Material/object that is a poor conductor.

**Ion** A charged particle produced by the loss or gain of electrons.

**Ionisation** Any process in which atoms become charged.

**Isotope** Atom that has the same number of protons but different number of neutrons, i.e. it has the same atomic number but different mass number.

# J

**Joule (J)** The unit of energy.

# K

**Kilowatt (kW)** 1000 watts.

**Kilowatt-hour (kW h)** Electrical energy supplied to a 1 kW electrical device in 1 hour.

**Kinetic energy** Energy of a moving object due to its motion; kinetic energy (in joules, J) = ½ × mass (in kilograms, kg) × (speed)$^2$ (in m$^2$/s$^2$).

# L

**Light-dependent resistor** Device with a resistance that varies with the amount of light falling on it.

**Limit of proportionality** The limit for Hooke's law applied to the extension of a stretched spring.

**Line of action** The line along which a force acts.

**Line of force** Line in a magnetic field along which a magnetic compass points; also called a magnetic field line.

**Liquid** A state of matter.

**Live wire** The wire of a mains circuit that has a potential that alternates from positive to negative and back each cycle.

**Load** The weight of an object raised by a device used to lift the object, or the force applied by a device when it is used to shift an object.

**Longitudinal wave** Wave in which the vibrations are parallel to the direction of energy transfer.

**Long sight** An eye that cannot focus on nearby objects.

# M

**Machine** A device in which a force applied at a point produces another force at another point.

**Magnetic pole** End of a bar magnet or a magnetic compass.

**Magnification** The image height ÷ the object height.

**Magnifying glass** A converging lens used to magnify a small object that must be placed between the lens and its focal point.

**Main sequence star** The main stage is the life of a star during which it radiates energy because of fusion of hydrogen nuclei in its core.

**Mass** The quantity of matter in an object; a measure of the difficulty of changing the motion of an object (in kilograms, kg).

**Mass number** The number of protons plus neutrons in the nucleus of an atom.

**Maximise** Make as big as possible.

**Mechanical wave** Vibration that travels through a substance.

**Microwave** Part of the electromagnetic spectrum.

**Minimise** Make as small as possible.

**Moment** The turning effect of a force defined by the equation: Moment of a force (in newtonmetres) = force (in newtons) × perpendicular distance from the pivot to the line of action of the force (in metres).

**Momentum** This equals mass (in kg) × velocity (in m/s). The unit of momentum is the kilogram metre per second (kg m/s).

**Motor effect** When a current is passed along a wire in a magnetic field and the wire is not parallel to the lines of the magnetic field, a force is exerted on the wire by the magnetic field.

## N

**National Grid** The network of cables and transformers used to transfer electricity from power stations to consumers (i.e. homes, shops, offices, factories, etc.).

**Near point** The nearest point to an eye at which an object can be seen in focus by the eye. The near point of a normal eye is 25 cm from the eye.

**Neutral wire** The wire of a mains circuit that is earthed at the local substation so its potential is close to zero.

**Neutron** A dense particle found in the nucleus of an atom. It is electrically neutral, carrying no charge.

**Neutron star** The highly compressed core of a massive star that remains after a supernova explosion.

**Newton** The unit of force (N).

**Non-renewable** Something that cannot be replaced once it is used up.

**Normal** Straight line through a surface or boundary perpendicular to the surface or boundary.

**North pole** North-pointing end of a freely suspended bar magnet or of a magnetic compass.

**Nuclear fission** The process in which certain nuclei (uranium-235 and plutonium-239) split into two fragments, releasing energy and two or three neutrons as a result.

**Nuclear fusion** The process in which small nuclei are forced together so they fuse with each other to form a larger nucleus.

**Nucleus** The very small and dense central part of an atom, which contains protons and neutrons.

## O

**Ohm's law** The current through a resistor at constant temperature is directly proportional to the potential difference across the resistor.

**Ohmic conductor** A conductor that has a constant resistance and therefore obeys Ohm's law.

**Optical fibre** Thin glass fibre used to send light signals along.

**Oscillating motion** Motion of any object that moves to and fro along the same line.

**Oscillation** Moving to and fro about a certain position along a line.

**Oscilloscope** A device used to display the shape of an electrical wave.

## P

**Parallel** Components connected in a circuit so that the potential difference is the same across each one.

**Payback time** Time taken for something to produce savings to match how much it cost.

**Perpendicular** At right angles.

**Pitch** The pitch of a sound increases if the frequency of the sound waves increases.

**Pivot** The point about which an object turns when acted on by a force that makes it turn.

**Plane mirror** A flat mirror.

**Potential difference** A measure of the work done or energy transferred to the lamp by each coulomb of charge that passes through it. The unit of potential difference is the volt (V).

**Power** The energy transformed or transferred per second. The unit of power is the watt (W).

**Power of a lens** The focal length of the lens in metres. The unit of lens power is the dioptre, D.

**Pressure** Force per unit area for a force acting on a surface at right angles to the surface. The unit of pressure is the pascal (Pa).

**Principal axis** A straight line that passes along the normal at the centre of each lens surface.

**Principal focus** The point where light rays parallel to the principal axis of a lens are focused (or, in the case of a diverging lens, appear to diverge from).

**Principle of moments** For an object in equilibrium, the sum of all the clockwise moments about any point = the sum of all the anticlockwise moments about that point.

**Proton** A tiny positive particle found inside the nucleus of an atom.

**Protostar** The concentration of dust clouds and gas in space that forms a star.

## R

**Radioactive dating** The use of a radioactive substance to give information about the age of an object.

**Radio wave** Longest wavelength of the electromagnetic spectrum.

**Range of vision** Distance from the near point of an eye to its far point.

**Rarefaction** Stretched apart.

**Real image** An image formed where light rays meet.

**Red giant** A star that has expanded and cooled, resulting in it becoming red and much larger and cooler than it was before it expanded.

**Red-shift** Increase in the wavelength of electromagnetic waves emitted by a star or galaxy due to its motion away from us. The faster the speed of the star or galaxy, the greater the red-shift is.

**Reflector** A surface that reflects radiation.

**Refraction** The change of direction of a light ray when it passes across a boundary between two transparent substances (including air).

**Refractive index** Refractive index, n, of a transparent substance is a measure of how much the substance can refract a light ray.

**Renewable energy** Energy from sources that never run out including wind energy, wave energy, tidal energy, hydroelectricity, solar energy and geothermal energy.

**Repel** To cause to move apart.

**Residual current circuit breaker (RCCB)** An RCCB cuts off the current in the live wire when it is different from the current in the neutral wire.

**Resistance** Resistance (in ohms, Ω) = potential difference (in volts, V) ÷ current (in amperes, A).

**Resultant force** The combined effect of the forces acting on an object.

**Resultant moment** The difference between the sum of the clockwise moments and the anticlockwise moments about the same point if they are not equal.

## S

**Sankey diagram** An energy transfer diagram.

**Series** Components connected in a circuit so that the same current that passes through them are in series with each other.

**Short sight** An eye that cannot focus on distant objects but can focus on near objects.

**Simple pendulum** A pendulum consisting of a small spherical bob suspended by a thin string from a fixed point.

**Socket** A mains socket is used to connect the mains plug of a mains appliance to the mains circuit.

**Solar cell** Electrical cell that produces a voltage when in sunlight; solar cells are usually connected together in solar cell panels.

**Solar energy** Energy from the Sun.

**Solar heating panel** Sealed panel designed to use sunlight to heat water running through it.

**Solar power tower** Tower surrounded by mirrors that reflect sunlight onto a water tank at the top of the tower.

**Solid** A state of matter.

**Sound** A form of mechanical energy.

**South pole** South-pointing end of a freely suspended bar magnet or of a magnetic compass.

**Specific heat capacity** Energy needed by 1 kg of the substance to raise its temperature by 1 °C.

**Speed** Distance moved ÷ time taken.

**Split-ring commutator** Metal contacts on the coil of a direct current motor that connects the rotating coil continuously to its electrical power supply.

**Star** A large ball of gas in space that emits radiation.

**Start-up time** Time taken for a power station to produce electricity after it is switched on.

**Step-down transformer** Electrical device that is used to step down the size of an alternating voltage.

**Step-up transformer** Electrical device that is used to step up the size of an alternating voltage.

**Stopping distance** Thinking distance + braking distance.

**Supergiant** A massive star that becomes much larger than a giant star when fusion of helium nuclei commences.

**Supernova** The explosion of a massive star after fusion in its core ceases and the matter surrounding its core collapses on to the core and rebounds.

**Switch mode transformer** A transformer that works at much higher frequencies than a traditional transformer. It has a ferrite core instead of an iron core.

## T

**Temperature** The degree of hotness of a substance.

**Temperature difference** Difference in temperature between two points.

**Terminal velocity** The velocity reached by an object when the drag force on it is equal and opposite to the force making it move.

**Thermistor** Device with a resistance that varies with temperature.

**Thinking distance** The distance travelled by the vehicle in the time it takes the driver to react.

**Three-pin plug** A three-pin plug has a live pin, a neutral pin and an earth pin. The earth pin is used to earth the metal case of an appliance so the case cannot become live.

**Tide** Rise and fall of sea level because of the gravitational pull of the Moon and the Sun.

**Time period** Time taken for one complete cycle of oscillating motion.

**Total internal reflection** Occurs when the angle of incidence of a light ray in a transparent substance is greater than the critical angle. When this occurs, the angle of reflection is equal to the angle of incidence.

**Tracer** A small amount of a radioactive substance used to give information about a mechanical or biological system.

**Transformer** Electrical device used to change an (alternating) voltage. See also Step-up transformer and Step-down transformer.

**Transverse wave** Wave in which the vibrations are perpendicular to the direction of energy transfer.

**Turbine** A machine that uses steam or hot gas to turn a shaft.

## U

**Ultrasound wave** Sound wave at frequency greater than 20 000 Hz, which is the upper limit of the human ear.

**Ultraviolet radiation** Electromagnetic radiation just beyond the blue end of the visible spectrum.

**Useful energy** Energy transferred to where it is wanted in the form it is wanted.

## V

**Velocity** Speed in a given direction (in metres/second, m/s).

**Virtual image** An image, seen in a lens or a mirror, from which light rays appear to come after being refracted by the lens or reflected by the mirror.

**Visible light** The part of the electromagnetic spectrum that can be detected by the human eye.

**Volt (V)** The unit of potential difference, equal to energy transfer per unit charge in joules per coulomb.

## W

**Wasted energy** Energy that is not usefully transferred.

**Watt (W)** The unit of power.

**Wave** Disturbance in water.

**Wavelength** The distance from one wave crest to the next wave crest (along the waves).

**Wave speed** Speed of travel of a wave.

**Weight** The force of gravity on an object (in newtons, N).

**White dwarf** A star that has collapsed from the red giant stage to become much hotter and denser than it was.

**Work** Energy transferred by a force, given by: Work done (in joules, J) = force (in newtons, N) × distance moved in the direction of the force (in metres, m).

## X

**X-ray** High energy wave from the part of the electromagnetic spectrum between gamma rays and ultraviolet waves.